SENECA

MEDEA

MASTERS OF LATIN LITERATURE

EDITORS: FREDERICK AHL, DISKIN CLAY,
DOUGLASS PARKER, JON STALLWORTHY

This series aims to help reestablish the importance and intrinsic interest of Latin literature in an age which has rejected the Latin literary model in favor of the Greek. We plan to make available, in modern English-language versions, influential Latin works, especially poetry, from the third century B.C. to the eighteenth century of our own era. By "influential works" we mean not only those commonly read in the classroom today, either in the original or in translation, but also those which shaped literature in their own and in subsequent times, yet have now either lost or been dismissed from their places among the "Great Books" of our culture.

SENECA

MEDEA

TRANSLATED AND WITH

AN INTRODUCTION BY

FREDERICK AHL

Cornell University Press

ITHACA AND LONDON

First published 1986 by Cornell University Press.
Second printing, with corrections, Cornell Paperbacks, 1996.

International Standard Book Number 0-8014-9432-x
Library of Congress Catalog Card Number 86-47635
Printed in the United States of America
*Librarians: Library of Congress cataloging information
appears on the last page of the book.*

☏ The paper in this book meets the minimum requirements of the American National Standard for Information Sciences—Permanence of Paper for Printed Library Materials, ANSI Z39.48-1984.

paper: 10 9 8 7 6 5 4 3

To the memory of Kathleen Mary Cain Ahl

Ní chuala mé in aird sa bhith
ceol ba binne ná do cheol
agus tú fá bhun do nid

Contents

General Introduction

Seneca's Life

Lucius Annaeus Seneca was born in Córdoba, Spain, shortly before the traditional date for the birth of Christ, around 1 B.C., to a family famous and influential in both politics and literature. He was the son of another Lucius Annaeus Seneca (the "Elder"), some of whose works, the *Controversiae* or *Exercises in Persuasion*, survive. His brother, Annaeus Mela, was father of the poet Lucan (Marcus Annaeus Lucanus), author of the *Pharsalia*, an epic poem which tells of the civil wars between Julius Caesar and his military and ideological opponents. Another brother, Lucius Iunius Novatus Gallio (so named because he was adopted by Iunius Gallio), is mentioned in Acts 18:12–18 as the proconsular governor of Achaea in Greece who refused to hear the Jews' case against Paul.

Early Christian writers were aware that the founders of Christianity and the famous philosophical and political family of Seneca were contemporaries. Tertullian describes Seneca as "often one of us,"[1] and there even survives a forged correspondence between Seneca and Paul, full of mutual praise in rather awkward Latin.[2] People found it hard to believe that the world of the Annaei and that of the Christian missionary, which touched in so many ways, should not have pro-

[1] *On the Soul* 20.
[2] C. W. Barlow, ed., *Epistolae Senecae ad Paulum et Pauli ad Senecam (Quae Vocantur)* (New York, 1938). Despite the forbidding title, the text is both in Latin and in English translation.

9

duced literary contact, especially since Paul and Seneca both fell victim to the emperor Nero. Paul and, traditionally, other disciples were put to death by Nero during his purge of the Christians in the aftermath of the great fire at Rome (A.D. 64). Similarly, Seneca and members of his family— Gallio, Mela, and Lucan—were all suspected of involvement in a plot to kill Nero the year after the fire (A.D. 65) and obliged to commit suicide.

Although Seneca, like many intellectuals of the first and second centuries A.D. (including his severest ancient critic, the rhetorician Quintilian), was of Spanish origin, he spent most of his life at Rome under the Julio-Claudian imperial dynasty. He was born in Augustus' reign, held his first major political office under Tiberius (A.D. 33), and was a famous orator by the time Caligula succeeded to the throne (A.D. 37). Although his success apparently excited Caligula's jealousy, it was not until the first year of Claudius' reign (A.D. 41) that Seneca first experienced the force of imperial displeasure. He incurred the wrath of Claudius' wife, Messalina, who procured his banishment to the island of Corsica. His recall did not come until A.D. 49, when Claudius' ambitious fourth wife, Agrippina, arranged for him to be tutor to her son, Nero, who became emperor in A.D. 54.

With Seneca's recall in A.D. 49 began the period of his greatest political influence, an ascendancy which lasted until at least A.D. 59, and, in a more limited way, until A.D. 62. Thereafter, Nero appears to have become increasingly suspicious of him. Distrust came to a head with the disclosure of the plot against Nero (A.D. 65), in which Seneca's nephew Lucan apparently played a major role. With the detection of the plot came the downfall not only of Lucan and Seneca, but of most of Seneca's circle of family and friends.

Seneca's Works

Most surviving Roman writers can be handily categorized either as poets or as authors of prose works. Seneca is unusual in that both poetic and prose works attributed to him have survived from antiquity. The poetic works that have come down to us under his name are one historical drama, eight tragedies, which we will discuss shortly, and some epigrams in the *Latin Anthology*. In prose he wrote twelve books of *Dialogues*, the lengthy essays *On Clemency* and *On Benefits*, 124 letters to his friend Lucilius, seven books of *Natural Questions*, and a satire on the death of Claudius, the *Apocolocyntosis*—"*Pumpkinification*." In these works, Seneca portrays himself as a member of the Stoic school of philosophy, though he frequently cites with admiration—and uses—ideas from rival intellectual groups, notably the Epicureans. Seneca's openness to ideas from different philosophical schools makes an interesting contrast with the hostility other philosophical writers of the first and second centuries A.D. show towards their intellectual opponents. To give two illustrative examples: The closest surviving ancient parallels to Seneca's satirical *Apocolocyntosis* are probably the *Dialogues of the Gods*, written by the Greek Epicurean Lucian a century or so later. Lucian is not nearly so kind to the Stoics, however, as Seneca is to the Epicureans. He mocks them mercilessly. Similarly, the closest parallel to Seneca's famous treatise *On Anger*, included among the *Dialogues*, is Plutarch's *On Anger*. Plutarch, however, had no patience with Stoicism and wrote two stinging essays, along with extensive negative comments elsewhere, attacking what he considered the absurdities of Stoic philosophy: *On Stoic Self-Contradictions* and *Against the Stoics on Common Conceptions*.

I mention these points because scholars sometimes interpret Seneca's poetry not just in terms of the Stoic elements in his philosophical prose, but as if he were an embodiment of the fundamentalist puritanism we find in Lucian's Stoic caricatures. They thus discover in his tragedies a kind of drama of Stoic dogmatism which accords ill with Seneca's—and Stoic—eclecticism, and with the Stoics' preoccupation with paradox. Yet even if we choose to believe Seneca was a Stoic zealot of the sort Lucian mocks, we do not have to see him as a soul that is self-confident and at spiritual peace. The religious and philosophical agonies of Milton or, no less poignantly, Donne, should warn us of the terrible "laceration of mind," as Samuel Johnson calls it, with which deep-seated religious feelings and conversions are associated. The same John Donne can, in other moods and times, produce the erotic flippancy of *The Flea* and the melancholy religious brilliance of *A Hymne to God the Father*. Similarly, Seneca will sometimes assure us of the invincibility of good, at other times confront us with the apparently inevitable triumph of evil.

11

The believer may struggle for footing over an abyss of atheism that the conventionally pious or the mere agnostic cannot begin to comprehend. Indeed, the eclecticism of Seneca's prose works might even emanate from the tolerance born in one who has experienced the agony of the abyss. Plato's Socrates in *Republic* 8–10 recognizes and fears the force of evil within the soul, the beast that awakens when the rational part of the mind is asleep. This irrational element, the mythical beast, must, he felt, be suppressed in each of us just as poetry must be suppressed within the state, at least in part because it gives form to the nightmarish and irrational. But to argue for the suppression of a passion or of an artistic form is to acknowledge one's fear of its power.

Seneca, unlike Plato, gives us two separate visions: the rational, philosophical obverse of his paradoxical coin and the poetical reverse. In fact, it is hard to be sure which side is the front and which the back of the Senecan coin. To get the complete picture, we must of course consider both. Nonetheless, it is entirely possible to contemplate each face separately. Students of Senecan philosophy have had no qualms about omitting discussion of the tragedies. Poets, therefore, have a precedent for the same sort of omission, but in reverse. We will, I would argue, gain a better picture of Seneca's poetry—and perhaps of his prose too—if we consider his tragedies, at least at first, *apart from* his prose works. For to do so will help us counteract a widely held but usually false assumption that poetry begins its existence as prose, and is, essentially, no more than a kind of ornate prose.

The manuscript tradition of Seneca's tragedies aids our task. For the plays, in fact, survived from antiquity separately from the prose works. Centuries ago it was thought that the poetry and prose were the works of two distinct persons: a tragic Seneca and a philosophical Seneca. So the question naturally arises: How do we know that the tragedies and the prose works were written by the same hand? Quintilian's quotation of *Medea* 354 in *Instructing the Orator* 9.2.8 is the only evidence that someone named Seneca actually wrote any of the plays that have come down to us under this name. Quintilian's phrase, "like Medea in Seneca," shows that (a) Seneca wrote it. But Quintilian may mean the Elder Seneca, as he clearly does later in the same chapter (9.2.42).

Settling the Senecan authorship of *Medea* still leaves unresolved the question as to whether the other nine plays included in the Senecan corpus are also by a Seneca. There is general consensus that one, *Octavia*, is not his work, and serious doubts have been raised about another, *Hercules on Oeta*. Most scholars accept the authenticity of the remaining seven—*Hercules in His Madness, Trojan Women, Phoenician Women, Phaedra, Oedipus, Agamemnon*, and *Thyestes*—even though, as we have seen, none of them is attested as Senecan by an ancient writer. I accept the judgment of scholars on the matter of the plays' authenticity, though I have a nagging suspicion that the *Elder* Seneca wrote *Phaedra* and, possibly, other plays.

Dating the Plays

Seneca is one of only a handful of Romans of senatorial rank before the fourth century A.D. who have survived to us as poets in their own right. Curiously, his most notable fellow aristocratic poets are his near contemporaries: his short-lived nephew Lucan (A.D. 39–65), author of the *Pharsalia*, and Silius Italicus (A.D. 25–101), author of the *Punica*. Like Lucan, and unlike Silius, Seneca appears to have written poetry while he was politically active. Yet Seneca differs sharply from Lucan as well as from Silius in several major respects. To begin with, they wrote epic, the most "elevated" of Roman poetic forms, and their epics show the self-confident moral and historical judgment that characterizes Roman senatorial writing. Their style is evocative of the aristocratic historians Sallust and Tacitus. They write of Rome itself, they lament the passage of a pluralistic, republican state. One is always aware of their Romanness and of the age in which they are writing.

Seneca, in contrast, not only chose tragedy, a literary form that had, by his time, ceased to be a major vehicle of poetic or political statement, but seems calculatedly to have avoided specific references both to his own day and to things Roman. Among the ten plays attributed to him, only *Octavia* deals with a contemporary subject. And few scholars now claim that this play was actually written by Seneca. In fact, Seneca is a character in it.

With the exception, then, of the *Octavia*, the plays attributed to Seneca present so few overt and recognizably Roman elements that

13

we are startled when we come upon them. This lack of contemporary reference makes dating the plays virtually impossible. The prose works, in contrast, are of much more certain date, ranging from his *Consolation to Marcia* (included among the *Dialogues*) in A.D. 41 to his *Natural Questions* and *Letters to Lucilius*, both published between A.D. 63 and 65.

Although the traditional, mythical topics Seneca selects for his plays are as obviously appropriate to the world of the early emperors at Rome as the mythical epics written by Statius and Valerius Flaccus in the decades just after Seneca's death, Seneca affords us no clues, as Statius does, about when his work was written and about what contemporary experience it refracts. We can hardly move beyond generalization. True, Seneca's plays, with the possible exception of *Phaedra*, mirror a top-heavy Roman world of absolute power as surely as Athenian tragedy mirrors the often chaotic Greek democracy and intellectual pluralism of Athens in the fifth century B.C. But, as Seneca lived his whole life under the imperial autocracy, we have not said much when we have said that.

Since dating the plays on external evidence and internal contemporary commentary is impossible, the best we can do is establish some probable sequence of their composition on the basis of internal stylistic considerations, as John Fitch has done.[3] Fitch accepts the general dating of *Hercules in His Madness* to before 54 B.C. This was the year of Claudius' death and Nero's accession to the throne. And one of Seneca's own works, the *Apocolocyntosis*, "*Pumpkinification*," parodies a lament from *Hercules in His Madness*. Fitch's study suggests that *Trojan Women* and *Medea* belong to approximately the same time period and that *Phaedra*, *Oedipus*, and *Agamemnon* are earlier. How much earlier, however, we cannot say. The fragmentary *Phoenician Women* and *Thyestes* were, according to Fitch's analysis written later, during the last decade of Seneca's life.

If Fitch is right—and there is no certain means of telling whether he is or not—Seneca's plays were written at various points throughout his life, but most *before* Nero's reign.

---

[3] "Sense-Pauses and Relative Dating in Seneca, Sophocles, and Shakespeare," *American Journal of Philology* 102 (1981): 289–307.

Critics and Admirers

Seneca was one of the most influential political, intellectual, and literary figures whose works survive to us from antiquity. He shaped the development of the tragic drama in Renaissance Europe, he inspired and influenced literary and intellectual figures as different as Montaigne and Calvin. In short, his appeal to creative writers has been immense. Yet the reader of modern articles and books about Seneca is more likely to encounter unfavorable than favorable critical evaluations of his work.

Hostility to Seneca is hardly new. From his own day on, Seneca's work and character have endured severe attacks from what we might loosely term the academic establishment. Writing less than a generation after Seneca's death, the rhetorician Quintilian takes him to task for a variety of errors in judgment and in style: the researchers he employed made mistakes; Seneca himself used "unnatural" expressions and strove to achieve a kind of terse "quotability." Seneca was, it seemed, a dangerous and potentially corrupting influence on a schoolboy's style of writing. Quintilian's reaction to Seneca was so strongly negative that some of his contemporaries thought it arose from personal loathing—an allegation Quintilian feels constrained to deny in his *Instructing the Orator*. The Roman historian Tacitus, writing shortly after Quintilian, passes similarly scathing judgment on Seneca's character: he was a hypocritically pious moralist with bloodied hands who lacked the courage of his convictions.

The negative scholarly view of Seneca did not gain the upper hand until the last two centuries, however. For the preceding millennium and a half, Seneca retained his following outside the classroom. Indeed, it was his enormous popularity as a literary figure in Quintilian's day which prompted the scholar to treat him at length, and in a special category apart from other writers, as a subversive literary model. After the early nineteenth century, however, Seneca lost his wide and admiring audience. Quintilian's anxieties about Seneca's corrupting influence were echoed by many Latin teachers who chose to instruct their students in the prose style of Caesar and Cicero and in the verse of Horace and Vergil. These teachers, too, found Seneca a corrupting influence who did not fit, and therefore undermined, firmly held notions of what a classical author should be both stylistically and morally. Seneca, like Apuleius and Statius, had to be rejected, however important he may have been in shaping Western literature, because he was "late," decadent, and "not classical." He did not represent the kind of Latinity, the period of Roman history, or the perspective on the Roman world that academics wanted to teach. And Seneca's critics found in Quintilian and Tacitus stylistic and moral justification for rejecting him.

Nineteenth- and twentieth-century scholarly antagonism to Seneca proved more damaging than Quintilian's attacks precisely because Seneca had lost his wider audience outside academia. It is important to understand, however, that his diminished popularity was not testimony to a change in literary tastes, as is sometimes suggested, but to the fact that Latin literature as a whole had become increasingly the exclusive and dwindling domain of academics who often seemed curiously determined to show how distasteful most of it was while lamenting that people were neglecting it. No field of literary study rivals that of Latin poetry in so systematically belittling the quality of its works and authors. And no field of literary study more thoroughly quarantines itself from contemporary critical thought. As a result, in many colleges Seneca is outside the still decreasing canon of academically "approved" writers, as are the overwhelming majority of ancient writers whose works are extant but unread even in excerpts.

Latinists often forget how many of the "faults" for which they denounce Seneca and other Roman writers are, in fact, the usual goals towards which poets and essayists strive: to make the language their own rather than to follow scholastically prescribed usage; to avail themselves of all the resonances of meaning their language can bear; to achieve the memorable, the quotable. The criticisms directed against Seneca by Quintilian and his successors could even more justifiably be leveled against Shakespeare: he, too, made mistakes in research, used "unnatural" expressions, and strove to achieve terse "quotability."

But recently the picture has been changing. Major critical editions of Senecan tragedy by Tarrant (*Agamemnon, Thyestes*), Fantham (*Tro-*

jan Women), and Fitch's forthcoming *Hercules in His Madness* and Costa's smaller *Medea* have begun to focus classicists' attention on Senecan drama. And although—or rather because—Seneca has ceased to be canonical reading, interest in his works, especially in his tragedies, has gradually reawakened among poets, historians of the theater, and Shakespearean critics. The ascendancy of what scholars and directors alike have taken to be the Greek model of tragedy became so marked and ubiquitous by the middle of the twentieth century that the Greek muse was no longer exotic. Sophocles seemed familiar. The Roman Seneca now became the remote, primitive, and mysterious writer. Roman tragedy had been absent from the canonical reading of our culture long enough for its rediscovery to be exciting and artistically stimulating. It was "other," it was malleable, it was the stuff of experiment and innovation in the theater. And that, Ted Hughes observed, is why Peter Brook wanted to produce Seneca's, not Sophocles', *Oedipus* in London at the Old Vic in 1968.

The differences between Senecan and Athenian tragedy are often—as they were to the producers of Ted Hughes' adaptation of Seneca's *Oedipus*—precisely the strength and theatrical allure of the Latin dramas. As Hughes wrote in his introduction to *Oedipus*, "the Greek world saturates Sophocles too thoroughly: the evolution of his play seems complete, fully explored and in spite of its blood-roots, fully civilized. The figures in Seneca's *Oedipus* are Greek only by convention: by nature they are more primitive than aboriginals.... Seneca hardly notices the intricate moral possibilities of his subject."[4]

I do not much agree with Hughes' assessment of Senecan as opposed to Sophoclean drama, since I believe that Sophocles, no less than Seneca, has been distorted by the puzzling modern desire to treat tragedies as moral and religious sermons. But this disagreement is beside the point. Hughes' essential point is, I think, correct: Senecan tragedy is vastly and intriguingly different from Greek tragedy. To contend that Seneca is doing no more than rendering some extant or nonextant Greek original is to do him the injustice that scholars have finally, I hope, stopped doing Plautus. The contrast, then, between Hughes' notion of Senecan tragedy and the conventional scholarly

---

[4] *Seneca's "Oedipus,"* adapted by Ted Hughes (London, 1969), p. 8.

view of Seneca could hardly be more total. Hughes is delighted that Seneca is un-Greek; classicists are upset that Seneca is not Greek enough.

Seneca's characters are more introspective and self-analyzing than even a Sophoclean Ajax. Their most critical battles, like the critical battles of many a Shakespearean character, are often those that they fight with themselves. Senecan drama constantly takes us beyond a character's words into his or her very thoughts, keeping us aware of the tension between what someone says and does and what that same person perceives as the reason for what is said and done. We see a character's hopes, illusions, and delusions played out before us.

Seneca and the Theater

Increased theatrical interest in Senecan tragedy contrasts with scholastic insistence that Senecan tragedy was never actually staged at Rome. We will never know if and how Senecan tragedy was staged. It is probably correct that Seneca's *Oedipus* was not produced before the massed citizen body of Rome as Sophocles' *Oedipus* was produced before the citizen body of Athens. But this does not mean it was not designed for performance and actually performed in small gatherings, as we shall see. Much modern drama is not aimed at, or performed before, a broad national audience either. Despite the accessibility of mass audiences through television and cinema, the contemporary writer often chooses to address a literary elite in a small theater.

Although Seneca clearly writes for an elite too, his plays deal with and direct themselves towards the powerful, as most modern theater in the English language does not. Senecan tragedy, like Greek, is about power and about those who exercise it, and it addresses the issues of power through the language of myth. It does not name contemporary names; it speaks through traditional characters drawn ultimately from an ancient poetic tradition whose roots extend back into the second millennium B.C. and beyond. Yet the fact that Senecan tragedy deals with and directs itself to the powerful is the reason it can be seen not only to resemble classical Greek tragedy but, paradoxically, to differ from Greek tragedy when one inspects it more closely.

During the Athenian democracy, poetic expression was dominantly theatrical. The Athenian audience that listened in the theater voted in the assembly; poets, like the popular leaders, sought to reach it and persuade it. Roman poets of the early empire, and those of pre- and post- democratic Greece, directed their work to the literate ruling classes, and shied away from "popular" drama. First, the populace had no political power in imperial Rome. It could not even vote to elect magistrates. That is why I find the Chorus' remarks in *Phaedra* 982–984 perplexing. Its words seem to suggest that the populace exercises a political role which it did not in Seneca's day:

> fraud rules as despot   in halls of power,
> the people find joy   in giving high office [*fasces*]
> to a vile man. They   adore those they hate most.

Second, under the Roman emperors it was difficult and dangerous, as well as, apparently, futile, to communicate with the popular audience. If a popular audience detected a covert insult or jest at the emperor's expense, it might be unsophisticated enough to roar its recognition, approving or disapproving, aloud—to the great peril of the writer. Smaller, more refined audiences, meeting in times of tyranny and in gatherings where names are known, react more cautiously. Experience teaches them that to acknowledge the insult or the jest, or even to be present when it is made, imperils the listener as well as the author. That is why, in a notorious incident mentioned by the biographer Suetonius in his life of Seneca's nephew Lucan, the people in a public restroom fled when Lucan, while breaking wind noisily, quoted a half-line written by the emperor Nero.

Besides, the literary theater never enjoyed in Rome the official state support it had in Athens. There were no permanent theaters until Pompey built one in 55 B.C. And that great general built it to give himself, not dramatists, a stage. Actors, as well as some playwrights, were often slaves or former slaves, not members of a fashionable profession. Further, dramatists had to compete for the public's attention with spectacles of increasing scale and extravagance that were underwritten by the wealthy and sanctioned by ritual practice. The Latin word *munus*, suggesting a public offering or service, came to be shorthand for a gladiatorial "offering." Such ritual and circus-like

19

entertainments were features of Roman life from the middle of the third century B.C. on. The ruling classes stressed the spectacular and underplayed the verbal and intellectual dimensions so fundamental to Greek drama. Terence, the comic playwright, in the prologue to *The Mother- in-Law*, says it was impossible to hold one's own against the competition of a tightrope walker. Holding one's own against a gladiatorial "offering" would have been no easier.

The poet Horace, writing in Rome a generation or two before Seneca, tells Octavian, the imperial Augustus, that Democritus—"the laughing philosopher," as he was called—would guffaw at the notion that a dramatist could win the attention of his restive audience: "he would think the writers were creating their play for an ass—and a deaf one. What voices have had power enough to overwhelm the noise which echoes round our theaters?" (Horace *Epistles* 2.1.199–201). Pleasure, Horace adds, has "shifted from the ear to eyes that are not good at seeing" (*Epistles* 2.1.187–188), even among the Equestrian order, the Roman upper middle class. And, he continues in the lines immediately following, not only games but triumphal processions celebrating military victories have intruded upon the dramatist's stage.

Horace' last comment has a special pungency in this epistle, addressed as it is to Octavian, who had been the victor in a savage civil war and was the conqueror and imperial ruler of Rome. If the biographer Suetonius is right in his claim that this poem is Horace's response to Octavian's complaint of exclusion from Horace's *sermones*, his "conversations"—the works we know as his *Satires* and *Epistles*— Horace is suggesting that the emperor, as principal giver of games and sole giver of triumphs, has usurped the dramatist's place in the theater. The theater is owned by the emperor and stages only his shows. Hence Horace's expressed desire to entrust himself to a *reader* rather than to a spectator (*Epistles* 2.1.214–218). The language and metaphor he uses are more appropriate to the arena and the hippodrome than to the muses and god of poetry. They suggest that Octavian thinks more in terms of a *munus*, "offering," than of poetry itself. He wants books that will fight for him like gladiators, that will serve his glory. The theater already exists for the emperor's glory; the threat lurks that all literature will come to serve the same purpose.

For Octavian now wishes to intrude himself into the poet's private "conversations."

Octavian was, in fact, more eager to censor published and *durable* poetry than the more fleeting criticism which might occur in a public performance. Ovid, who died in exile when Seneca was in his teens, chastises Octavian for being so concerned about morality in poetry but so unconcerned about the blatant immorality of what is represented in the theater and at the emperor's own games, before his very eyes (*Tristia* 2.497–546). In *Tristia* 5.7.25–30, Ovid comments on the irony of his own situation in this regard: some of his poetry has been adapted for and performed in the theater, although he himself claims: "I have—and you know this yourself—written nothing for the theater." Incidentally, if we take Ovid at his work here, the two lines said to have survived from his play *Medea* would seem either not to be genuinely his or to be adapted from his treatments of Medea elsewhere in his poetry. He may, of course, have written the work for reading or performance elsewhere than in the public theater. Still, in his exile, he says, he takes some consolation in the thought that his poems, adapted for the theater, keep his memory and name alive in Rome.

The theater, then, was seen by both poet and political leader in the generations preceding Seneca not only as a noisy place, unconducive to poetry, but as a vehicle of corruption and political propaganda. Succeeding Roman emperors, particularly Nero and Domitian, were also well aware of the theater's power. Domitian banned actors from the public stage. Nero adopted a much different approach. Part of his own immense popularity—and much of the contempt that men of letters felt for him—stemmed from his appearances as a performer in the theater and the hippodrome.

Despite their reluctance to write for the popular stage, Roman writers were aware—in Ovid's case poignantly aware—that performances in the theater have a power over the popular imagination that "pure" poetry lacks, and they regularly presented human activity in terms of the theater or amphitheater. In his *Aeneid*, Vergil describes the landscape of North Africa as a *scaena*, a stage set, and compares the nightmarish visions of Queen Dido to the horror experienced on stage by Pentheus or Orestes. When Aeneas visits the new Troy built by Andromache, he walks in on a tragic tableau: a mock Troy frozen in time, as if in a painting or stage set, with Andromache lamenting, as ever, over an empty grave honoring her dead husband, Hector. The characters of Latin poetry also see themselves theatrically or amphitheatrically. In Lucan's *Pharsalia*, Pompey, builder of Rome's first permanent theater, dreams of his past triumphs in theatrical imagery. As he dies, he behaves like an actor who must win approval for his final scene. Lucan, in fact, gives an important role in the *Pharsalia* to the man who invented the amphitheater: Scribonius Curio. And this Curio, we are told by the historian and naturalist Pliny, a contemporary of Seneca's, was the same man who maneuvered the opposing political factions of the Roman state into civil war, much as he turned his two back-to-back theaters into one amphitheater to stage a grand gladiatorial contest.

Seneca presents life in terms of the arena both in his tragedies and in his philosophical works. In his essay *On Providence* he dismisses ordinary gladiatorial shows as "the childish delights of human vanity" and asks us to contemplate instead the greatest contest of them all: "a matched pair worthy of god's eyes—a brave man pitted against an evil destiny, with the brave man as challenger." In his tragedies, particularly *Trojan Women*, many motifs suggest a theater far different from that of Aeschylus or Euripides. The site of Polyxena's sacrifice on Achilles' tomb, for example, is described as if it were part of a *munus*, an offering, in the amphitheater (*Trojan Women* 1123–1126):

> on the other side,
> it [the tomb] is encompassed by a plain, rising
> gently at the edges to create
> a valley in between—the shape suggests
> a theater, in fact.

Astyanax' death has much the same "theatrical" quality. The dramatist asks his audience and readers to envisage the scene from Greek myth in terms of the familiar horror of ritual death in the Roman theater. And he asks them to censure those who hated what they saw but watched anyway. Roman readers could hardly fail to see themselves reflected in the Senecan mirror, much as they would see themselves in the equally stinging comment in the passage from *Phaedra*, cited earlier, that they worship those holders of the *fasces* (the Roman symbols of public office) whom they hate. Yet Seneca is aware that he, like his morally critical messenger, is himself as guilty of hypocrisy as those he criticizes.

At least one of Seneca's tragic characters, the messenger whom I would identify with Talthybius in *Trojan Women*, recognizes how sacrificial and gladiatorial death affects the spectator: desire to watch vying with hatred of what one watches. Seneca understands that part of his audience will see the victims as heroic and that such heroism is beyond words. The doomed Polyxena in *Trojan Women* does not speak; Astyanax says only "Pity me, mother." In the verbal environment of tragedy, the sacrificial heroes themselves do not speak. They, like the Chorus envisaging cosmic catastrophe in the *Thyestes*, invite the listener or reader to imagine, not to hear. Seneca, like other great writers of Roman imperial times, often creates images for the mind's eye rather than for strictly visual perception.

The model that Seneca's Roman reader or listener used as his imagination wandered could be drawn from memories of the countless silent "performers" who died each year at Roman games. This same amphitheatrical notion of heroic death helped the growth of Christianity. The martyrs who died in the arena recalled the secularized contests to their ritual origins. And the horror of their suffering fixed another myth in men's minds.

To interest a popular Roman audience in a stage "death" when the games afforded ample opportunity to see real death must have been difficult. The dramatist could not compete, and probably would not have wanted to compete, with the grim spectacles Martial, a poet of the generation after Seneca, describes in his *Book of Spectacles*. The Roman amphitheater imparted to even the grossest and most grisly myths a certain air of reality. The emperor Titus staged not only Hercules' labors at the games in real-life performances but the consummation of the Cretan queen Pasiphae's obsessive passion for a bull. Pasiphae was the wife of Minos, king of Crete, and she was helped in her desire to mate with the bull by the Athenian artist Daedalus, who designed a cowsuit for her to wear so that the bull would mistake her for a heifer. Her child by this union was, of course, the famous Minotaur:

Believe it now! Pasiphae did make it with the Cretan bull;
  We've seen it happen; the old story now has credibility.
Yet ancient folklore should not take the credit for itself:
  Caesar, your circus actors make *all* folksongs live for you.

In the following poems Martial reiterates his point about the "realization" of myth on stage. Poem 7 is the culmination of the series.:

Just as Prometheus, bound tight on a Russian crag
Fed with his ever-healing and regrowing heart
The bird that never tires of eating
                              So,
                              cast as Laureolus,
The bandit-king, nailed to a cross (no stage-prop this)
The unknown actor showed his raw guts to a Highland bear.
His shredded limbs clung onto life although
Their bits and pieces gushed with blood:
No trace of body—but the body lived.
Finally he got the punishment he deserved . . . [5]
  Maybe he'd slit his master's throat, the thug;
  Maybe he'd robbed a temple treasury of gold, mad fool;
  Maybe he'd tried to burn our city, Rome.
The criminal responsible surpassed all ancient folklore's crimes.
Through him what had been merely myth became
  Real punishment.

The condemned criminal—whose crime, we note, no one seems to know for sure—is condemned to act out the role of Laureolus, the bandit-king, crucified in the arena.

The cruelty Martial describes was not Titus' invention. Titus was merely continuing a tradition begun by the emperor Caligula. Suetonius, the biographer of the earliest emperors, describes the bloody competition for the role of Laureolus in Caligula's day in his *Life of Caligula*. But what Martial sets first in our minds is the myth of Prometheus: the benefactor of mankind, enduring the daily attacks of the bird that fed on his liver and knowing the secret that would

---

[5] Part of the line is lost in our texts.

24

bring about the downfall of his tormentor, the god Jupiter. The comparison with the man playing Laureolus, then, horrifies with its appropriate inappropriateness. Myth tells us how Prometheus offended Jupiter, but it also reassures us of his ultimate release by Hercules. Martial's nameless criminal, however, guilty of crimes unknown, will have no Hercules to free him, and a wild bear, not a surgically precise bird's beak, will torment him. The poor substitute Laureolus, whatever he did, earns the status of Prometheus, which, in this incident, gives him a greater claim to divinity than any of the emperors who often pretended that they were themselves gods: Jupiter incarnate. Martial's Laureolus walks the same "stage" as the suffering Christ.

Martial, the poet-artist, does not specifically thank his emperor for this demonstration of myth's viability (as he thanks him in each of the preceding poems), surely because the poem is a terrible indictment of what his eyes have seen and thus of whoever it was that organized the grim spectacle. Martial had some reason to be cautious. For, as poem 8 makes clear, the artist himself may endure a similarly mythlike fate:

> Artistic Daedalus:
>> When you were being wolfed and mangled by that bear
>> How you must have wished you now had your wings!

Daedalus, having helped Pasiphae mate with the bull, later designed the labyrinth to conceal her child. He also helped Theseus kill the beast and escape with Minos' daughter Ariadne. Understandably, he lost his royal master's favor. Minos imprisoned him in his own work of art. Daedalus escaped by inventing wings and flying out. Martial's latter-day Daedalus, however, out of favor with his Minos, has no wings to escape his enraged master and the carnivorous beast.

The Roman imperial poet's task was dauntingly Daedalus-like. Aware that he served an often cruel master, he had to communicate without ending up like Martial's Daedalus. The poet knew he could not compete for an audience of the moment with the spectacle, with the reality of Roman theatrical death. He could not even express his full disgust with that spectacle, his horror at it—much less attempt to aid its victims—without risking a terrible fate himself. In the first

25

satire of Juvenal, a near contemporary of Martial, we are told of a critic whose charred corpse inscribes a black line in the sand of the theater after he has been used as a human torch to light the arena. The poet risks being transformed from a writer into a pen with which others write. Hence, perhaps, his flight from and fascination with the theater, his preference for epic and for myth. As Martial shows, only myth could express the extent of the horror of what was happening precisely *because* even myth paled in comparison with the staged reality. Life, as presented in the arena, had become an imitation of art. Ovid, in his *Metamorphoses*, suggests it always had been.

Staging the Plays

Senecan tragedy demands performance, not just recitation by two or three readers. The rapid interchanges between, say, Medea (or Phaedra) and her nurse need actors, not just voices. The commonly held view that the plays were recited by a single voice assumes that the Latin terms *recitare* and *recitatio* carry the same sense as the English "recite" and "recitation." There is no reason, however, to suppose that they preclude the notion of performance by multiple actors, much as *recitare* does in Italian theatrical parlance. *Recitare un dramma* means "to perform a play," not "to recite a play." What is sometimes called the "Recitation theory" of Senecan tragedy owes much both to this restrictive Anglo-German-French sense of what *recitatio* must have been and to the low opinion scholars hold of Senecan tragedy as theater. Many Latinists, I am sure, would agree with Elaine Fantham's observation that Seneca's tragedies "are not well-crafted stage-plays."[6] I disagree. Having staged three of the plays, and served as an adviser in the production of a fourth, I have been surprised at how effective they are as theater. Scholars exaggertate the difficulties of staging them and undervalue their theatrical innovations, perhaps to justify their view of the tragedies as one-man recitations.

None of the complete plays attributed to Seneca presents major staging problems to a director, much less difficulties comparable to

[6] *Seneca's "Troades": A Literary Introduction with Text, Translation, and Commentary* (Princeton, 1982), p. 49.

those found in such Greek tragedies as Sophocles' *Ajax* or Aeschylus' *Eumenides* (which *were* publicly performed). Once we accept Senecan tragedy as designed for performance, we may appreciate better some of the remarkable effects, actual and potential, in the staging of *Phaedra*, *Medea*, and *Trojan Women*. In *Trojan Women*, for instance, Seneca brings Pyrrhus onstage to take Polyxena away to be sacrificed. Pyrrhus and Polyxena move but do not speak. Yet they are spoken to by Hecuba and Andromache. In forceful contrast, Hecuba and Andromache, though they speak, are not involved in the *action* of the scene.

Yet if, as I have suggested, the plays were designed for performance but not performed in public theaters, were they only plays in search of a stage, or were they performed but in a less public manner? The germ of an answer is found in Suetonius' *Domitian* 7. Domitian, we are told, "forbade actors to use the [outdoor, public] stage, but conceded to them the right to practice their art indoors." Domitian's action, of course, was taken some thirty years after Seneca's death. But the practice of "in-house" performances may well have been going on for some time before Domitian's decree. And this, I believe, is how Senecan tragedy was performed: in the more than ample homes of well-to-do Romans. I emphasize that my resolution of the problem is no more than a matter of personal opinion—as are other theories about the performance or nonperformance of the plays. I also warn the reader that stage directions given in the translations are only my suggestions. Recall, however, that stage directions found in translations of Greek tragedy are also the work of a translator—though he or she does not always acknowledge this to be the case.

Ultimately the question as to how Senecan tragedy was presented matters more to a historian of the theater than to a director. The real question for the director is whether he would find one of these plays stageworthy if he had a usable script in hand. And here is the major problem: there are few English versions of Senecan tragedy and even fewer which suggest that the plays are stageworthy. My aim has been to produce stageable versions of the plays without resorting to adaptation rather than translation and without sacrificing the poetry in an effort to achieve colloquial realism. For Senecan tragedy, like Shakespearean or Greek tragedy, is a poetic form, not just a dramatic one.

About the Translations

Translating Seneca is hampered not only by critical prejudice against the plays but by an increasing tendency to disparage Latin literature as a whole. Latin has been for centuries the language of learning and of pretentiousness. And, unlike Greek, its latter-day scholastic rival, it has a rather English appearance, since so many English words are derived either directly or indirectly from Latin. It is remote enough to appear abstract and pedantic but too familiar to seem exotic. If Erich Auerbach had called his book *Imitatio* rather than *Mimesis*, it would probably have had less appeal. To caricature the popular stereotypes: the Greeks, who were imaginative, practiced mimesis; the Romans, good at building arches but less adept at poetry and philosophy, practiced imitation. These stereotypes are well established in English-speaking societies. And Latinists themselves are largely responsible for them.

Although many English words look as if they should be equivalents for their Latin ancestors, they often differ greatly in meaning or "feel." We would rarely assume that the character of a remote ancestor can correctly be assessed by analyzing the character of a modern descendant of the same name. Yet we are sometimes less than cautious in making similar assumptions about English words of Latin ancestry. "Accept," for example, derives from the Latin *accipere*, which means something like "to take to oneself." The English "accept" lacks the aggressive sense of *accipere*. It comes from a passive form of the Latin verb and retains a sense of passivity, as do a great many words used in Latinate English. The lethargy of the descendants belies their ancestral vigor. Yet popular dictionaries and translations still use the descendants to represent their forefathers, largely because scholars cannot agree on alternatives. "Virtue," derived from *virtus*, is a good instance, especially because here we are concerned with a Roman writer who had much to say about *virtus*. Ancient Roman *virtus*, not out of place on the battlefield, evolved into the now obsolete "virtue" as philosophers, moralists, and monks adapted it for use in a sexual context.[7] At the beginning of the twentieth century Francis Cornford,

---

[7] "Virtue," in all likelihood, died when its own adjective, "virtuous," was found unacceptable by movie censors in Hollywood in the 1930s. Presumably virtue's foes

in the introduction to his translation of Plato's *Republic*, satirized the use of "virtue" as a translation for the Greek *arete*: "One who opened Jowett's version at random and lighted on the statement . . . that the best guardian for a man's 'virtue' is 'philosophy tempered with music,' might run away with the idea that, in order to avoid irregular relations with women, he had better play the violin in the intervals of studying metaphysics."[8] Subsequent Greek scholars have dealt with the problem not by seeking another equivalent but by adopting *arete* into their usage as a translation for itself. Latinists, in contrast, generally retain "virtue" for *virtus*. Those embarrassed by "virtue" yet fearful of scholarly scorn for using an English term which misses many nuances of *virtus* cautiously imitate the Hellenist and use *virtus* as a translation for itself. Such subterfuge is available to the scholarly commentator but not to the translator. And I have tried to avoid it. Obviously my choice, "manliness," will not please everyone. But it does try to bring out the force of *vir*, "man," in *virtus* even though it cannot catch the paradoxically feminine gender of the Latin original.

The translator must take into account other differences between Latin and English. Latin is compact and polysyllabic. English is more monosyllabic and far more compact. There are inevitably more words in an English sentence than in its Latin original, but not necessarily more *syllables*. I have tried to keep the number of syllables in my English approximately equal to the number of syllables in Seneca's Latin. Since the English iambic pentameter used here in place of the Latin trimeter is syllabically shorter, however, there are more lines in my English then in the Latin. For the reader's convenience, I mark the line numbers of the Latin original in the margins.

To convey the force and style of Senecan tragedy, something must be done with his ubiquitous wordplay. It is insufficient, when translating poetry, to select the word in language *A* which most closely approximates what scholars take to be the meaning of a given word

---

realized that if someone were described as "not virtuous," audiences would naturally assume that he or she was sexually active. Mention of sexual activity was taboo in English and American films of the period. The RKO studio therefore instructed its writers to avoid words which suggested physical sexuality, however obliquely. "Virtuous" was one of the words proscribed (as was "nursery"). See K. MacGowan, *Behind the Screen* (New York, 1965), p. 358.

[8] *The "Republic" of Plato*, trans. F. M. Cornford (Oxford, 1941), p. vi.

in language *B*. Poetic word selection is rarely governed exclusively, or even largely, by considerations of what teachers call "literal" meaning. Seneca, like many poets, ancient and modern, creates a richly allusive text where the "literal" meaning of a word often explodes into wordplay of multiple resonances suggested by the context in which it is set. I render the wordplays I have detected (puns, anagrams, and so forth) by equivalent plays in English.

My translations aim at a formal but not stuffy American literary and poetic idiom, interspersed, where appropriate, with a more colloquial style to underscore changes of mood and tone in the original. A few residual Anglicisms from my British childhood may have crept in too. At the same time, I have avoided such Americanisms as might appear stridently alien in other English-speaking countries. My usage may therefore seem synthetic and artificially neutral. I would defend my choices in these matters on the grounds that Senecan tragedy is itself formal in style and diction, and in verse. The tragedies are poetry and cannot be transposed satisfactorily into modern, colloquial prose drama without radical departures from the structure of the original.

I found that each Senecan play had a very individual "feel." The characters are quite distinct from one another even when they have similar roles. Thus the nurse in the *Phaedra* and the nurse in the *Medea* are as distinctive as the protagonists they serve. Indeed, no preconception about Senecan drama strikes me as more fundamentally incorrect than the notion that each play is essentially a variant of one plot, rehashed with characters of a dull sameness. As I translated, what surprised me most was the ironic wit of such characters as Pyrrhus and the humorous yet horrifying pomposity of Agamemnon in the *Trojan Women*. It had not occurred to me before that Seneca, like Euripides, might be capable of enhancing our sense of horror by evoking laughter.

My approach to each play is different, partly by design, partly by accident. The elaborate choral metrics of the *Phaedra* seemed to need a more elaborate English response than the delectable but less complex metrics of the *Trojan Women*. So I chose to approximate the Latin meters more closely in the *Phaedra* than in the *Trojan Women*. On the other hand, I prepared these translations over a period of some fifteen years, finishing the *Trojan Women* first and the *Phaedra* last. During that period my approach to Latin poetry and translation has changed considerably. But I have tried not to edit out my earlier perceptions of the *Trojan Women*, my personal favorite among the tragedies. I believe it to be the finest piece of theater Seneca produced, comparable with the best of Greek drama.

Questions the Plays May Prompt

Seneca clearly assumed that his audience or readers were intimately familiar with Greco-Roman myth. To help the reader less familiar with these tales, I have prepared brief introductions to the myths underlying each play and appended a glossary. Where the translation makes an important but indirect allusion to a character or place, I have noted at the foot of the page the glossary entry under which the information can be found. Sometimes, of course, ancient writers made statements or allusions which were probably as obscure to their contemporaries as they are to us, and were probably intended to puzzle or stimulate thought. These questions I have not attempted to answer in the text, but have left for the reader or performer to resolve.

A play, let us remind ourselves, is like a musical score in that it does not really live until it is performed. And then it has as many potentially different forms as it has directors, actors, and critics. So in the individual introductions to the plays I have sketched some questions the reader may want to ask about the characters and their roles. Characters in good drama, as in real life, are not simply linear, consistent beings (as scholars sometimes try to make them). They behave differently in different situations. They contradict themselves, they are often torn between conflicting impulses and obligations. Senecan drama is much more firmly rooted in the conflicts within the individual mind than are most Greek tragedies. Understanding the characters and the play involves a search for those areas or—to use a geological metaphor—those faults where different segments of a personality threaten each other and, in a larger sense, the stability of the world about them.

The Latin texts of the tragedies used are, in general, those of Elaine Fantham (*Seneca's "Troades": A Literary Introduction with Text, Trans-*

lation, and Commentary [Princeton, 1982]), C. D. N. Costa (Seneca, *Medea* [Oxford, 1973]), and P. Grimal (*L. Annaei Senecae Phaedra*, Erasme, Collection de textes latins commentés 14 [Paris, 1965]). I am grateful to Wolfgang Haase and the de Gruyter Press for giving me permission to reuse a few pages of my article "The Rider and the Horse: Politics and Power in Roman Poetry from Horace to Statius," *Aufstieg und Niedergang der römischen Welt* 32.1 (Berlin/New York, 1984), pp. 40–110. And I owe many debts to the friends and scholars who have given me advice and criticism: John Fitch, Eleanor Winsor Leach, Elaine Fantham, David Konstan, Joan Jeffri, David Keller, Rajani Sudan, and to my classics students and colleagues at Cornell, the University of Otago in New Zealand, and the University of Texas at Austin who helped me stage them. Sincere thanks also go to Martha Linke and Georgia Nugent, who saved me from many errors; my fellow editors of the Masters of Latin Literature, Diskin Clay, Douglass Parker, and Jon Stallworthy; above all, to my wife, Mary.

MEDEA

Introduction to *Medea*

Seneca's *Medea* is one of two surviving ancient tragedies of Medea. The other is Euripides' rather different play of the same name.

Play and Myth

Medea, whose name in Greek means "the woman who plans or plots," is the child of Aeetes—himself the child of Sol, the Sun—and of Idyia (a daughter of Ocean), whose name means "the woman who knows." Medea's homeland is Colchis on the eastern shores of the Black Sea, a city on the Rioni River (called the Phasis in antiquity). Colchis would have been the easternmost limit of Greek navigation before the age of Alexander the Great. In several ancient versions of the myth, Medea's aunt is Circe, who lives on an island called Aeaea, identified with various places near the *western* limits of Greek mythical navigation.

Medea, like Circe, has magical powers. And, like Circe, she becomes the lover of a Greek sailor—Jason, son of Aeson, king of Iolcos (modern Volos), in the Greek territory of Thessaly. Circe's lover, of course, was Odysseus (Ulysses in Roman writers). But in all mythic versions the relationships of the two sorceresses to their lovers differ. The most striking differences are these: Jason, a bachelor, marries Medea and brings her, an alien, back to his Greek world before he abandons her in favor of a Greek wife. Odysseus (Ulysses), already married to Penelope, never attempts to take Circe from her homeland. Odysseus and Circe part on apparently good terms, but Jason's abandonment of Medea arouses Medea's fierce resentment and passion for vengeance.

Medea meets Jason when he comes to Colchis in quest of the Golden Fleece—a symbol of royal power that Pelias, his uncle, ordered him to bring back to Greece from the Black Sea. Pelias had treacherously deposed Jason's father, Aeson, but tells Jason that if he brings back the fleece, he will let him become king of Iolcos. The Golden Fleece had been taken from a magical ram, sacrificed in Colchis after it conveyed a fugitive pair, Helle and her brother Phrixus, across the Aegean and towards the Black Sea. Helle, the story goes, drowned in the narrow straits at the entrance to the Black Sea, but Phrixus sailed on to Colchis. Tradition has it that the Hellespont was named for the lost Helle.

Jason sails in quest of the Golden Fleece in a ship, *Argo*, endowed with magical powers. It could, among other things, speak prophetically. Jason was helped in his voyage by a magnificent crew of gods and demigods, known as the Minyae or Argonauts. Among those mentioned or alluded to in *Medea* are Orpheus, the famous poet and singer; Idmon and Mopsus, two prophets; Lynceus, famed for his excellent vision; Tiphys, the *Argo*'s helmsman; the sons of the north wind, Zetes and Calais; and—though present for part of the voyage only—Hercules. But dominating the Chorus' recollections of *Argo*'s crew is its sense that *Argo*'s voyage was an act of trespass upon the sea, punished—or destined to be punished—by the subsequent suffering of each individual sailor.

Among the nautical dangers encountered by the Argonauts and mentioned in this play are the Sirens, whose singing lures sailors to death upon the rocks; Scylla, a monster, part woman, part beast, who devours sailors; Charybdis, a whirlpool that sucks ships down beneath the waves; and the Symplegades or Clashing Rocks, which threaten to crush passing vessels. But obtaining the fleece itself (once he comes ashore at Colchis) is Jason's most difficult personal ordeal—one he would have been unable to survive without the aid of Medea and her magic. King Aeetes requires him to perform a series of apparently impossible tasks before he can take the fleece. He must yoke a pair of fire-breathing bulls, plow a field, and sow it with a dragon's teeth. From the teeth will sprout warriors fully armed that Jason must dispose of. Medea, who falls in love with Jason, helps him accomplish these labors and also puts to sleep the dragon guarding the tree on which the Golden Fleece is kept. In return, Jason promises to take her back to Greece with him.

When Jason has procured the fleece, he and Medea elope. Medea also takes her young brother Absyrtus along. Aeetes, enraged, pursues them. To hold off his pursuit, Medea kills Absyrtus and scatters his limbs behind her. Aeetes, whose fatherly concern makes him stop to pick up the limbs, fails to catch the fugitives, who eventually make their way back to Thessaly.

Upon his return to Iolcos, Jason demands that his uncle Pelias surrender the throne, as previously agreed. But Pelias refuses. Thereupon Medea takes a terrible revenge with her magical powers. In the presence of Pelias' daughters she dismembers an old ram and boils it in a cauldron with magical potions. The old ram emerges whole and rejuvenated. Medea persuades Pelias' daughters that they can restore their father's youth in the same way. But of course they lack Medea's magic, and Pelias dies horribly. Yet his death does not bring Jason the throne, which falls instead to Pelias' son, Acastus. Jason and Medea (now parents of two children) must flee to avoid Acastus' revenge. They seek asylum in Corinth.

Creon, king of Corinth, is happy to receive Jason, whom he sees as a suitably famous husband for his daughter Creusa, but he wants nothing to do with Medea. Jason agrees to leave Medea and marry Creusa. Medea is to be banished. It is at this point that the play begins.

Notes and Questions about the Characters

Medea Medea's mood vacillates greatly in this play. But although there is a schizophrenic quality about her, she quite often gives the outward appearance of being controlled, even seductive. In conversation with both Jason and Creon she makes frequent use of sexual innuendo. Why?

From early on we see she does not want Jason killed. Does she still love him? She certainly attempts to negotiate with Creon so he will give her back both Jason and the *Argo*, and she even asks Jason to join her in flight. In the first two acts we may easily imagine that Medea would be content with some action against Creon and Jason's new wife. But the contrast she makes between the crimes she committed before she had children and the crimes she ought to commit now that she has given birth inevitably bring her own children into her thoughts of vengeance. At first they are simply to be the bearers of deadly gifts to Creon and his daughter. Later they are to be her means of punishing Jason. He loves the children and will sacrifice her for them. So she will sacrifice the children to punish him and, in a curious way, regain her independence from him. After she has killed the first of her two children, she declares that her virginity is being restored. Does she think she is somehow reversing time, regaining innocence?

One part of Medea responds with humane instincts and seems sympathetic to the experiences and sufferings of others, and is in frequent conflict and dialogue with the other part, which is enraged with a sense of injury, fired with a desire for vengeance, and proud of its criminality. But then, how human *is* Medea? She has, of course, been living as a woman, and she has the powers of a sorceress. But there is something godlike in her which gives her power to escape through heaven in a serpent-drawn chariot. If she is a god, however, she makes nonsense of Jason's final claim that her presence is evidence that gods do not exist. (Consider, by the way, that in the Latin text *gods* is both the first and the last word of the play.)

Jason It is easy to see Jason as the caricature of a coward since he is is so far removed from the self-assertive male hero. But is it fair to do so? Even Medea, early in the play, asks herself what else Jason could have done. We learn from Creon's opening lines that it was Jason's prayers which caused Creon to change his mind about killing Medea. (*Could* Medea be killed?) So there is some reason to credit Jason's claim that only his intercession saved her life. But is it a misuse of heroic language to talk of conquering someone by prayers, as Jason says he does? Note that he approaches Medea in the same way: he hopes to conquer her by prayers too.

Seneca's Jason is aware of his moral dilemma, aware that he is not treating Medea rightly; the only self-justification he offers is that love for his children, not fear for his life, makes him abandon Medea. Does Medea believe this assertion? Does she kill the children because she knows Jason loves them, and is Jason in earnest when he offers to let her kill him in place of his surviving child? Why does Medea not take Jason up on his offer to die in place of the remaining child?

Creon Creon wants to deal with Medea indirectly, through his servants. He is clearly afraid of her, wants her gone from his kingdom, yet is susceptible to being maneuvered by her suggestions that he will prove himself a tyrant if he does not give her a hearing. Why? His demands that Medea leave his kingdom and "liberate my citizens from fear" curiously echo a famous speech by the Roman orator Cicero (who died in 43 B.C.) against Catiline, a noble who was plotting to overthrow the state. A Roman reader would not have missed this echo. You may speculate as to why Seneca included it.

Nurse Nurses in ancient tragedy may either dominate the women they advise or be dominated by them. The nurse in *Phaedra* falls into the first category. The nurse in *Medea* falls into the second. Lie low, behave meekly, run away: such is her advice. Yet she knows well enough what Medea has done in the past. Why does she doubt Medea's power now? Is her role mainly to accentuate Medea's lack of fear of the politically powerful? Does she ever attempt to discuss the morality of an action with Medea (as Phaedra's nurse does with Phaedra)?

CHARACTERS

MEDEA	daughter of king Aeetes of Colchis; rejected wife of Jason
NURSE	servant, compatriot, and confidante of Medea
CREON	king of Corinth who granted Jason and Medea asylum, and who is about to marry his daughter to Jason
JASON	husband of Medea and nephew of Pelias, king of Thessaly recently killed with Medea's help; leader of the naval expedition on the *Argo* which captured the Golden Fleece
MESSENGER	
MEDEA'S TWO SONS (nonspeaking)	
CHORUS	Corinthian people
VARIOUS ATTENDANTS (nonspeaking)	

41

ACT I

The curtain rises to reveal Medea, *alone in the courtyard of her house in Corinth, praying before a shrine of the gods. In the background music can be heard: singing, in celebration of* Jason'*s wedding to Creusa.*

Medea: Gods who couple men and women, listen!
Lucina, listen, bright guardian of birth,
midwiving children from the womb.
                                 Pallas,
you taught Tiphys to guide the first vessel,
Argo, so it could master a straight course,
making itself at home upon the seas,
now straits themselves.
                        Hear me.
                              Neptune, vicious
enough to master Ocean's heaving threats,
I pray to you.
                     And you, Titanic god,
marking and making day with blazing eye
of light.
                You too, perceptive Hecate,
governor of heaven, hell, and earth,
illuminating rituals that are,
and should be, secret,
                    I appeal to you.

I call those gods upon whose names Jason
swore his oaths, names Medea might
more rightly spell in prayer.
                  Hollow oneness

Titanic god: Sol

of eternal night, realms faced away   10
from life above, ghosts in chains, dripping
loathsome murder.
                        Ominous master
of those realms of horror, hear my prayer,
my hideous prayer.
                        You too, Proserpina,
ominous mistress, carried off like me
but not abandoned, treacherously left.

Powers of feuding vengeance, snakes writhing
repulsively upon a single head,
come to me now. Grasp the black fires of death
in ghastly hands dripping blood, and stand
menacing, as when I married him.
Kill his new partner, kill his new father,
snap all the royal family's living shoots.

For the groom, may something worse remain.
I want him to live: to wander through   20
cities as yet unknown, his confidence,
his livelihood destroyed; a refugee,
frightened and with nowhere to call home,
looked on, if he's looked upon at all,
with hatred; a notorious would-be guest,
seeking shelter in someone else's house.
I pray he'll wish we were together still.

I now request the worst prayer of them all:
that the children show the qualities
of their father and their mother combined.
My final vengeance is already born:
and I have given it birth.
                        But I'm sowing

Ominous master: Dis
Powers of feuding vengeance: Erinys, Furies

seeds of verbiage, complaints that have
no harvest. I will tear wedding torches
out of their hands, I'll tear the very light
out of the sky. Sol, the Sun himself,   30
sowed my family's seed, yet watches now
impassively, and lets himself be watched,
firmly keeping to his usual,
solitary course through open space
and the pure fire of heaven. He does not
return to his own rosy birth, unmake
this day.
        Shining father, give me control,
let me drive the coupled power of fire.
Then Corinth's Isthmus, double boundaries
of land dividing seas, delaying ships,
could be consumed with flames, the twin seas joined.

One thing remains. I long to bear the torch
blazing before them to the bridal suite,
to make the sacrificial prayers, butcher
the beasts on consecrated altar-stones.
If, my soul, you have some force of life,
if traces of your fabled energy
still linger on, seek out an opening   40
so you can penalize them, ruthlessly
slicing through their guts as if through wax.
You must banish from yourself all fears
a woman has. Take on your native mind,
your Cossack mind, that hates all foreigners.
Whatever criminal acts the Crimea,
Rioni River, and Black Sea have seen
the Isthmus soon will see. Evil actions
of brutality unknown—enough
to send shivers through heaven and earth alike.
That's what the mind within me urges me

---

coupled power of fire: Chariot of the Sun

to bring upon them: slashing butchery,
roving death, approaching limb by limb.

I am wasting time. I did all this   50
in virgin innocence. Some fuller pain
should rise within me now I've given birth.
People expect it. Medea, bare your rage
for fighting, and prepare yourself to kill,
work to a frenzy. When tales of your life
are told, men will, I hope, pair your divorce
with your wedding in well-matched rivalry.

When you leave him, your trail will be the same
as once it was when you pursued him here.

Delays damp fire. So break them off. This home
was quickened and born in crime. Quickly
and criminally must I leave it now.

(*The* CHORUS *enters, chanting for* JASON *and Creusa's wedding, and moving toward* MEDEA's *house.*)

Chorus: This is a wedding of kings   and so we hope
gods, kings of sky above   or bounded sea,
will come, responding to   the people's prayers.

A white-skinned, radiant bull,   neck carried high,   60
should honor the powerful gods,   the Thunderers.

A body, female and virgin,   snowy white,
pleases the goddess who brings   life to light.

Love, busying War's hands   bloodstained and rough,
giving the nations truce   from death and strife,

---

roving death: See Absyrtus
Thunderers: Jupiter and Juno

you store inside your horn   fertile riches.
Your prize for gentleness: sacrifice tender.

At legal weddings you,   Hymen, scatter
shadows of night with fire: a good omen.
Step lurching this way,   merry with wine,
crowning your temples with   wreaths of roses.   70
Light of temporal twinning,   evening star,
always too late for lovers,   twilight hour:
greedily mothers and brides   yearn for you,
and the moment you prick the sky   with brightness.

Her virgin luster conquers,   when compared
to Athenian brides, or Spartans   limber and lithe,
mountain-exercised   like boys
in a wall-less stronghold.   Lovelier she
than girls bathed in crystal   Alpheus,
washed in waters of   Aonia.   80

If Aeson's son, Jason,   let judges' eyes
assess his looks, gods would   concede first place.
Bacchus in tiger chariot,   lightning-born,
and great prophetic Phoebus   brother of
heaven's taut huntress-virgin   would give way.
Pollux, with castigating fists   concedes;
Castor as well, his match,   except with gloves.

Gods of heaven, I pray   I pray you: let   90
this woman conquer,   surpass other wives;
let this man rise far   above other men.

When she stands among women at the dance
her face alone outshines all others there.
So stars fade and die before the sun,
so flocking Pleiades coyly hide

---

huntress-virgin: Diana.

when Moon's arched horns, with mirrored brightness,
complete a whole and sunlike circle.
So whiteness drenched in Punic crimson   100
blushes red; so shepherd, rosily
glistening in the new day's light, sees
the gleaming crest of sunrise surging up.

Bridegroom, raped from a Tartar's bed,
afraid, yoked to a wife unbridled,
unsolaced by unwilling daily
contact, reap virgin fruit, the daughter
of the wind. This is your first time too—
first time with full parental consent.

Come, lads. Your songs can be a little lewd:
Bounce your lyrics anyway you want.
Rare's the chance for free speech against kings.

Bacchus' child, white-robed Hymen who carries the
        thyrsus!
Time to inflame the piny torch's myriad fibers!   110
Whip up that solemn fire with fingers no matter how
        listless!
Let us speak out our jest in style ribald and Italian.
Leave the crowd free for farce.
                                We consign to silence
        and darkness
any woman who runs from home, wedding-veiled for
        an alien husband.

(*Exit* CHORUS, *laughing and mocking* MEDEA.)

---

reap virgin fruit: Creusa
thyrsus: See Bacchus
Italian: See fescennine

ACT II

Medea: My twilight before night; my urge to kill.
The wedding hymn pounds at my ears; and still
I find it hard to grasp that this evil
is really happening.
                    How did Jason
find the power to do it? First he took
my father and the country that we ruled
away from me. Now he casts aside
the seeds of my existence—ruthlessly
left in solitude on foreign soil
to wither. I have earned better than this.   120
He's seen me mastering the energy
of fire and water, yet he despises me.
Can he suppose my power to inflict
evil is totally burned to ash?

I'm sick at heart; I can't see what to do.
My mind is ravaged by insanity,
I'm torn to pieces, scattered everywhere.
What source can I tap for vengeance now?
He doesn't have a brother, I regret;
but he does have a wife. So into her
my knife will go. Yet this is not enough
for what I've suffered. There must be some crime
that cities, Greek or savage, do not know,
something your hands have never tried before.
You must devise it, your past crime must spur
you on, it must come back to you, it must.

The Golden Fleece, symbol of royal power: 130
recall how it was torn away, recall

49

the tiny boy who followed his sister,
sheared from himself, limb by limb, butchered
as an act of war against father,
his body scattered upon open sea.
Recall the limbs of Pelias, himself
an old man and a father, boiled in bronze.
So often when I've been the cause of death,
the blood that's spurted has been kindred blood.
Yet I have never killed in anger. Love
makes me destroy.

But Jason had no power,
and surely did not plot this by himself;
he too was foreign under Corinth's laws.

He owed it you to steel himself for death,
not steal away.

Don't say that, please, oh please,
raging voice of my pain. Jason must live,   140
be mine, just as he was, if he has strength;
even if not, I still want him to live,
and to remember me. I don't want him
to hurt the gift of life I gave him once.

Creon's to blame. He uses royal power,
his only potency, to cast off ties
that bind together marriage partnerships,
to separate a mother from her sons.
He tears up pledges that should be intact.
It's solely his responsibility,
and he alone should pay due penalty.
Go after him! I will bury his home
in ash and cinders; Malea will see
this citadel in black against the flames,
Malea, whose arching promontory
holds fast ships of war with long delays.

---

tiny boy: Absyrtus
his father: Aeetes

Nurse:	Silence, I beg you. Hide your grievances. 150
	Mute them to fury locked within yourself.
	Endure without a sound wounds that cut deep,
	and bide your time. Maintain a level head;
	then you will have the power to repay.
	Your anger hurts when it is camouflaged;
	if you proclaim your hatred, it will lose
	the space it needs for vengeance, and the time.

Medea: Your pain has little bite if it retains
the power to reason and conceal itself.
Great sufferings do not lurk in disguise.
It is a pleasure to retaliate.

Nurse: Stop it, my child. Aggressiveness is mad
when even stillness of body and tongue
scarcely protects you.

Medea: Pluck up courage; then
Luck fears you. But she crushes all cowards.

Nurse: Test her when there's a place for manliness. 160

Medea: Place can't deny itself to manliness.

Nurse: There is no hope to light your pathway there.

Medea: If one is strong enough never to hope,
there is no reason to abandon hope.

Nurse: The Colchians have gone. Your partner's oaths
are valueless. You once had everything,
but nothing now survives to stand by you.

Medea: Medea still stands. In me you see
the energy of earth and water, fire,
steel, the gods, and heaven's vengeance.

Medea

Nurse:	Beware the king.
Medea:	My father too was king . . .
Nurse:	Don't armies frighten you?
Medea:	I do not care if they sprout up like harvests from the earth.
Nurse:	You'll die.
Medea:	I wish I would.
Nurse:	Run!
Medea:	I have run enough, and I'm ashamed.

170

Nurse:	Medea . . .
Medea:	Yes, I shall become Medea.
Nurse:	But you are a mother . . .
Medea:	And you see the kind of man who made me one.
Nurse:	Yet still you hesitate to run away?
Medea:	Oh, I will leave. But first: revenge.
Nurse:	Then vengeance will follow you.
Medea:	I'll find a good excuse to slow it down.

Nurse:　　Hold your wicked tongue! You've lost your mind!
Less insolence now, less talk of teaching
lessons. Honor allows us to adjust
to what a situation demands.

Medea:　　Fortune has power to ferret out my goods
but not my spirit.
　　　　　　　Somebody's pounding
the palace door. I hear it opening:
Creon is here, in person, swaggering
with blue-blooded Hellenic arrogance.

(*Enter* CREON, *with* ATTENDANTS. *As he comes in,* ME-
DEA *holds her ground in center stage.*)

Creon:　　(*Stopping with displeasure and fear when he observes that*
MEDEA *has not yet left.*)
Medea! That murderous child of Aeetes,
King of Colchis! Has she not yet removed　　　180
herself from my domains? Mill-like, her mind
works on inexorably, grinds and refines.
Her treachery leaves its mark; so does her hand.
Will she leave anyone alive or safe
from fear of butchery?
　　　　　　　Swift action,
to wipe out the disease her presence brings:
this I was planning. But my son-in-law
conquered my better judgment with his prayers.
She was allowed to live. Now she may go
in safety. Let her free my land from fear.
(MEDEA *approaches* CREON *slowly and steadily with eyes
fixed.*)
Beastlike, aggressive, threatening, she stalks
towards me to converse now face to face.
Keep her away! Don't let her touch me, men,
don't let her near me. Tell her not to speak
a word. Sooner or later she must learn
to tolerate imperial commands.

(CREON'S MEN *retreat before* MEDEA'*s advance, leaving*
CREON *to confront her himself.*)
Go away! Yes, run away, take flight,   190
take your hideous viciousness away,
so I don't have to look on it again!

Medea: What crime, what act of immorality,
          brings sentence of exile as punishment?

Creon: That's for an innocent woman to ask.

Medea: If you're the judge, then hear my cause and case;
          if you're the king, just tell me your commands.

Creon: You will obey the king's commands, however
          just or unjust their balance may be.

Medea: Justify power's balance, or it falls.

Creon: Complain in Colchis. Go!

Medea: I'm going back.
          But let the man who brought me take me there.

Creon: Your appeal's too late. Sentence is passed.

Medea: The man who passes sentence without hearing
          the defense: his ruling may be just—
          agreed. But he has not himself been just.   200

Creon: Did you give Pelias a hearing when
          you put him to death? Still, here's your court.
          State your peculiar case. Regale us now.

Medea: When I lived regally in my own right,
          I learned how hard it is to redirect
          one's energy of mind from anger once
          anger is aroused. I also learned
          that those who so ambitiously reach out

for power's regalia think that to pursue
unswervingly the policies that took
their fancy at the outset is the heart
of all true government.
      True, I am now
a pitiable sight, annihilated
by total disaster. I asked mercy;
I was thrown out. Sole and friendless,
I was deserted. Waves of misfortune
have washed me down. Yet, on my father's side,
I was illustrious. Like lightning,
I gleamed. For I derive the brightness of
my origin from my grandfather, Sol,
the Sun itself. Those fields gently winding
Rioni stiffens to harvest, all   210
the Black Sea looks upon towards the east,
this, with the glitter of regal power,
my father rules. There the bitter sea
is sweetened by fresh water, there women
are only kept inside the natural bounds
made by the Thermodon. They need no men.
And when they band together for a fight,
they need no armor to protect themselves
and rout their enemies out of their land.
Nobly born, I promisingly flowered;
I gleamed in the regalia of power.
Princes then begged to marry me; but now
I must beg them. For fickle Luck has wrenched
my charm away. She swooped down, she tore me
from my throne, dropped me in banishment. 220
Trust in your royal power, when fickle Chance
tosses great riches to and fro!
       Yet kings
do have a huge and marvelous resource
which time cannot destroy: the power to help
the suffering, the power to protect,

Luck: Fortune

not punish, those who beg mercy.
        The sole
resource and treasure I salvaged from days
of power in Colchis was precisely this.
I saved the glory of your race of Greeks.
The wondrous flowering beauty, sprung of gods
without me would have been by now erased.
Orpheus softens granite with magic
of song and makes the forests walk. He lives,
thanks to me. Castor and Pollux   230
are my gift, a double offering.
So too the twin sons, seed of the North Wind;
then Lynceus, whose penetrating sight
sees lands that lie beyond the Black Sea's shores.
I saved the lives of all the *Argo*'s crew.
Their king of kings I now omit. For him
you owe me nothing. I set no price on him.
The others I brought back for all of you;
this one alone I brought back for myself.
Come on, pile high against me in the scale
every moral outrage I have done;
I will confess to each. But the sole crime
I surely can be charged with is just this:
that I restored the *Argo*.
       A good girl's
pleasure should be in her virginity
and in her father's love. But let us see
what happens to The Past if I am good.
Your pure Hellenic land will go to ruin,   240
Why? All its leaders, don't you see, will die!
And first to fall will be your son-in-law,
seared by the flames from a raging bull's mouth.

Fortune may crush my case in any way
she likes. Yet having saved so many scores
of kings causes me no regret. I think
it glory. If my immorality
has brought me a reward, you are the one

with power to lay me down the terms for it.
If it takes your fancy, then condemn
the accused. But give me back the thing
I am accused of taking. I admit,
Creon, to guilt; for I create danger.
You well knew what I was when first I asked
for mercy at your knees, begged you to give
your hand as guarantee of your good faith.
Now I request some corner of a room
within your land, some squalid lair to hide
in misery. However, if you'd rather
drive me out of town, give me some place   250
that is remote, yet under your control.

Creon: No. I am not a man who brutally
and heavy-handedly wields royal power.
When I see misery, I am not proud;
I do not grind it underneath my heel.
I call as witness to this claim the fact
I married my child to a refugee,
a banished man, a beaten man, a man
quaking with abject terror. Acastus,
king of Thessaly, now wants him seized
and sent back for punishment and death.
This is his complaint. His own father,
he says, was killed—a man advanced in years,
almost senile, weak and prone to spasms.
He was butchered and his limbs were diced.   260
Acastus admits it was his sisters
who dared to carry out this ghastly act
of family murder. But he also claims
they did it as an act of family love,
deluded by your trickery.
                    A case
can be made for Jason if we keep
you clear of it. He took no part in this.
No drop of blood touched him. His hands were clean.
For they came nowhere near the instrument

of butchery. He kept his distance then,
unstained by any intercourse with them
or you. But you, the criminal mastermind,
combine a woman's boundless, brazen schemes
with a man's stamina. And your good name
is so long lost it lies beyond the power
of memory to recall.
                           Get out. Drain
this kingdom of its filth, and, as you go,
take all your poisons and your lethal herbs.   270
Liberate my citizens from fear.
Set up your house in someone else's land
and sunder there the peace of heaven above.

Medea: You force me to get out. Then give me back
my boat so I can leave, and give me back
my fellow traveler. Must my exile
be solitary? Why? My journey here
was not a solo venture. You're best off,
if you fear war, to drive out both of us.
Why draw the line between two criminals?
Pelias died for Jason's benefit,
not mine. Jason is why I went from home
and stole the fleece. For him I left father,
murdered my brother, mutilated him.
You can't blame me for what he taught and still
teaches his new wives to do. I've harmed
the many I have harmed not for myself
but because I have been made to harm.   280

Creon: You should have gone by now. You have waited
too long to sow delaying verbiage.

Medea: A final plea for mercy as I go:
my sons have done no harm. Don't let the sins
their mother has committed drag them down.

Liberate my citizens from fear: see Cicero

Creon: So go. I'll raise them with a father's love,
        as if I had begotten them myself.

Medea: Good omens for the royal wedding day
        and for its consummation. That's your wish.
        For you have hopes you want to see fulfilled,
        you want your royal powers to hold firm
        in spite of shifting Fortune's fickleness
        which harasses them.
                        Here is my plea:
        be generous. Just grant me a short delay
        in the enforcement of my banishment
        so I may be a mother to my sons,
        pay them the last, perhaps the dying, dues
        of love.

Creon: You mean you want time for a plot.   290

Medea: How can you fear a plot? Time is too short.

Creon: The evil hardly require time to harm.

Medea: A little time for tears. Can you deny
        this much to me in all my suffering?

Creon: Fear grafted deep inside me fights against
        you and your request; but nonetheless,
        a delay is granted so you can
        prepare for banishment—but just one day.

Medea: That is too much. Cut it back, if you wish.
        I'm in a hurry too.

Creon: You will be killed.
        No pleas for mercy will be heard unless
        you are gone from the Isthmus well before
        the Sun brings back the light of day. But now,
        the wedding sacrifices summon me.

I must participate. This day is marked
for Hymen and it summons me to prayer.   300

(*Exit* CREON *towards his palace and the wedding.* MEDEA
watches him go, then retires into her house. The CHORUS,
*moving on quietly, watching her as she withdraws into the
building, begins to meditate somberly.*)

Chorus: Far too audacious
was the man who first broke
through narrow waters
promising and faithless.
Though his raft was fragile,
he trusted life and
breath to shifting breezes'
gossip as he cut
over level waters,
out from his homeland.
Not knowing where his
voyaging would take him,
he dared to trust a
slender shell of kindling,
a much too thin line
laid down between the
passages of living
and those of dying.

No one yet knew stars
or used the constellations
painted upon the
sky's eternal brightness.   310
Shipping could not yet
survive by just avoiding
Hyades' rainstorms.
Then the stormy She-goat,
and Northern Wain, which

---

raft: Argo

Boötes slowly
follows like a herdsman,
were nameless, as were
north wind and west wind.

Yet Tiphys dared spread
canvas on the vast sea,
and write new laws for
winds to mock and follow: 320
how to run full sail,
how to catch the crosswinds—
haul in the for'ard sheet—
how to make the yards safe—
drop them down to midmast—
how to lash them topmast
when impatient sailors
pray for winds to rise,
when red streamers
flutter on the topsail.

Our fathers saw an
age of purest brilliance
when treachery was
far removed from mankind.   330
Men lazily kept
to their own shores, aged well
in the poor fields their
fathers tilled before them.
Still they were rich, though
knowing only that wealth
yielded by soil which
they themselves were born on.

Rightly the laws of
nature fenced the world off.
But *Argo* tore down
fences, made the world one.
She bade the seas be

lashed by sweeping oarstroke.
Seas: a dimension
once, and more, a boundary
of human fear, now
well within fear's limits.

Yet *Argo*'s pines from   340
Thessaly paid dearly
for acts of trespass,
steered through long–drawn terror.
Two mountains, great dams
sealing off the water's
surge from the deep sea,
rose from below, groaned loud
as heaven's thunder,
drenching the peaks and clouds
and then, in firm grip,
trapping the ocean.

Bold Tiphys blanched; he
loosed the hawsers he held;
silenced was Orpheus,
torpid grew his harpstrings.
Argo lost voice too.   350

Then there was Scylla,
virginal Sicilian,
madness' hounds en-
circling her womb; she
opened their great mouths
all at once. What sailor's
limbs did not stiffen,
totally in terror
at this one evil
mass of jaws all howling?

Two mountains: Symplegades
Argo *lost voice too*: see *Argo*

Then came destructive
sounds of singing softening
Italy's seas; yet
on his lyre Olympian
Orpheus from Thrace re-
sponded and resounded.
Usually a Siren's   360
song holds ships in her spell.
But now his music
prevailed, and almost forced her
to come in his wake.

What did this voyage
gain? A fleece of gold and
a fruit of evil
worse than the harsh sea brine:
it won Medea,
merchandise fit for
this, the world's first vessel.

By now the sea has
given up the struggle,
puts up with our laws:
we don't look for *Argo*s,
famous and seamed by
skilled hands of Minerva,
oars manned by monarchs.
Coracles and skiffs rove
at will on deep sea.
Boundaries have all moved;
cities now build walls
in lands just discovered.   370

Nothing is left where
once it was; the world is
open to travel.

---

destructive/sounds of singing: see Sirens

Medea

Indians quench their
thirst in cold Araxes,
Persians now drink from
Elbe and Rhine routinely.
There will come an age,
a distant Chinese year when
Ocean will lose its
power to limit knowledge,
and the gigantic
earth will open to us.
Tethys, sea goddess,
will disclose whole new worlds;
no more will Iceland
be our far horizon.

Enter MEDEA *hurriedly from her house, followed by her* NURSE.

Nurse:
My child, you leave the house so hurriedly.
Where are you going? Stay where you are! Put down
your anger and control your violent urge   380
to go on the attack.

(MEDEA *motions her to keep her distance and moves on down-stage, seething with anger.*)

Nurse:
(*inwardly*)   Like a woman
who has taken god into herself
upon the whitecapped mountain pinnacle
and the paired peaks of Nysa, she cannot
dam the madness, dashing to and fro,
a wild beast in her movements, and wearing
searing trademarks of insanity
upon her face. The sharpness of her glance,
blazing, startles the very soul in her,
shouts her secrets aloud, moistens and shines
her eyes with welling tears, mirroring every
twist of feeling.
              Now she is standing still—
threatening and heaving, howling, groaning.   390
Where will the crushing force of her intent
strike? When will it moderate its threats?
Like the sea her madness swells. When will
its moaning breaker crash upon itself?
What she turns over in her mind will be
no ordinary deed; she will surpass
her median of crime; she will conquer

65

herself. The moment I saw them, I knew
the ancient hallmarks of her angry rage.
Some enormity looms over us,
some bestial act of inhumanity.
I read upon her face the savage wish
to have revenge. I hope to god I'm wrong.

Medea: (*inwardly*)
Poor woman, if you ask what bounds to set
upon your hatred, imitate the cruel
limits that you placed upon your love.
Am I to tolerate this royal event,
endure the blaze of wedding torches, yet
not respond with vengeance? Shall I let
this day go by without my usual fire,
this day so intricately politicked   400
and engineered by both contracting sides?
While earth mediates the sky's balance,
while gleaming universal order rolls
in radiant waves of predetermined change,
while grains of sand are numberless, and Day
follows the Sun and Stars the Night, and while
the Great Bear never dips into the sea,
my passion for exacting punishment
will never cease but ever grow greater.
No monster of the land, no bitch Scylla,
no maelstrom of Charybdis sucking in
the seas of Italy and Sicily,
no volcanic Aetna which crushes   410
the gasping forces of the earth boils
with anger as destructive as my own.
Rivers in flood, the ocean churned by storms,
the Black Sea whipped to fury by the winds,
the violence of fire fanned by blast
from bellow have no power to stop the rush.
Did Jason fear Creon and the wars
threatened by the king of Thessaly?

---

the gasping forces of the earth: see Typhoeus

True love has power enough to fear no one.
But, granting him the benefit of doubt:
suppose that he was overwhelmed, gave in
and gave his hand. It certainly was still
within his power to come to his partner
if only for a final word or two.
Our lionheart was too frightened even
for this. As son-in-law, he certainly
did have the chance to ease the time limits   420
harshly imposed upon my banishment.
We have two children; I am given one day.
I'm not complaining that the time is short.
I can extend it farther. For this day
will brand its face of fire upon the world
so man will never lose its memory.
I shall attack the gods, and I shall shake
the elements.

Nurse: My lady, now your woes
make thoughts run riot. So, control yourself,
calm your mind.

Medea: My solitary chance
of calm comes when I see the elements
shattered with me as I fall. I want
the world to die with me. When you pass on,
there's joy in taking everything with you.

Nurse: If you maintain this course, how many forms
of retribution you must fear. No one
is powerful enough to make attacks   430
upon the powerful and still survive.

(*Exit* NURSE; MEDEA *withdraws backstage as she sees* JA-
SON *enter.*)

Jason: Fate is always hard, Luck hopelessly

---

king of Thessaly: Acastus

rough and—whether she devours us whole
or lets us go—impartially evil.
The remedies god finds are much too often
worse than the dangers that they save us from.
If I had wanted to make good the pledge
I gave my partner—and she's earned it, too—
my life would have been forfeit in exchange.
So, if I did not want to die, poor man,
my pledge to her had to be forfeited.
It was not fear that triumphed over pledge,
but an uneasy sense of what was due
my family. Once their parents were dead,
our children clearly would have followed us
on to the grave.

    If sacred Justice lives
above us in the skies, I call on it   440
to give approval and bear out my words:
my children forced their father to give in.
Although she has the heart of a wild beast,
and finds it hard to work in partnership,
under constraint, she will herself, I think,
prefer to act on her children's behalf
than to maintain her standing as my wife.
My mind's resolved to go appeal to her,
angry as she may be.
(*noticing* MEDEA)
       And she is here.
She's seen me and she's leaped out of the house,
burning with anger. Hate and every pain
that she has ever suffered are inscribed,
willful and vengeful, now upon her face.

Medea: We're on the run, Jason, we're on the run.
Not that moving home is new. Rather,
the reason we are moving home is new.
I'm used to being on the run solely
for you.
    I'm on my way. I *am* leaving.

You are compelling me to run away
from what is now your homestead in the sun.   450
You send me back.

             Where to?

                  Should I set out
for Phasis and Colchis, my father's realm,
the soil I watered with my brother's blood?
Do you tell me to head for somewhere else?
Where? What monstrous seas do you point out?
The Black Sea's jaws? Through them I brought back
    home
a fistful of kings, when I cut back
between the Clashing Rocks as I pursued
a roving lover.

           Iolcus, perhaps:
a little place—or, if in Thessaly,
should I head on to Tempe?

                  Everywhere
I've opened up a road for you, I've closed
one for myself.

            You send me back? Where to?
You order an exile into exile,
and don't provide her anywhere to go.
Well, let that pass. A king's new son-in-law   460
has ordered it. It therefore must be right.
Inflict upon me any penalty,
grim as it may be. I'll not resist.
My services must match what I am paid.
Your king can penalize his new son's whore
with all the blood and anger that he likes.
He may put her down and lock her hands
in chains, then he may seal her in with rocks,
and crush her in a never-ending night.
What I shall experience will be
far less than all the payments I have earned.

Thankless mind without a body: think.
Wind your thoughts back to your encounter with

the scorching breath of the flame-breathing bull,
the terror gripping you among people
never tamed. Think of Aeetes' herd,
their fire, in a field whose harvest was
steel-clad fighting men. Think of a foe
which sprouted without warning from the earth.
I bade them slaughter one another. They   470
sank back to death without a human word.
Throw on the fleece, plundered from Phrixus' ram,
and the nightmarish, vigilant monster.
I ordered him to shut his shining eyes
in sleep he'd never known. Think of my brother:
I put him to death: one child cut down,
but with how many cuts.

          My schemes took in
an old man's daughters. With deluded hopes
that he would be reborn, they carved his joints.

You have hopes for your children, for a place
to call your home.

          Remember horrors seen
and overcome, these hands which showed no pity   480
when employed for you.

          Remember too
the sea and sky that witnessed our mating,
and
    pity me.

          Return the debt you owe me:
give me life. In seeking power for others,
I threw my own away.

          My Scythians brought
plunder from distant lands as far away
as India with her burned and harried tribes.
Our house could hardly hold its great treasures,
it was so full. So we made living trees

---

vigilant monster: The dragon that guarded the Golden Fleece
old man's: Pelias

bow with loads of gold. From all this wealth,
I brought only my brother's limbs; and these
I spent for you. I gave up brother, father,
fatherland, and my virginity.
This was my dowry when I married you.
I want it back now that you run me out.

Jason: Creon wanted you dead; he hated you.   490
My tears crushed him. I won exile instead.

Medea: I see it now. Exile is a reward.
I'd thought it was a form of punishment.

Jason: Run while there's chance. Go, tear yourself away.
There's always harshness in a ruler's wrath.

Medea: You take Creusa's part with this advice.
She hates your mistress. So you move me out.

Jason: *Medea* judges morals and amours?

Medea: Premeditated murder . . . treason too.

Jason: Cite one specific charge against me now.

Medea: Whatever crime I did.

Jason: This is too much.
To be held guilty of your crimes as well.

Medea: They are your crimes, they're yours! You gained by
        them   500
so you committed them. I don't care if
the whole world holds your partner to account:
be her sole counsel for defense, sole voice
calling her innocent. If she's guilty
for your sake, for you she's innocent.

Jason:	I owe you my life. But when one is ashamed to stand in someone else's debt, it's hard to take that gift with gratitude.
Medea:	Ashamed? Don't take the gift then, give it back!
Jason:	Why don't you master your emotions, and, for the children's sake, calm yourself down?
Medea:	I renounce them. I deny they're mine, I swear them away. Why should I let Creusa supply brothers to my sons?
Jason:	As queen, she has the power needed to help the suffering children of us refugees.
Medea:	That will be an evil day for them, poor creatures, mingling shining families with base and low. So may it never come. May sons of Phoebus never mix with sons of Sisyphus.
Jason:	Poor woman, do you want to drag the two of us to banishment? Please go away.
Medea:	Creon heard my appeal.
Jason:	Tell me. What could I do?
Medea:	For me? Perhaps a crime.
Jason:	But how, with kings on either side?
Medea:	There's also something you should fear much more:

510

Kings on either side: Acastus and Creon

Medea. So set me against the rest,
let us fight it out; let Jason be
the prize.

Jason: I'm tired of evil. I withdraw.
You too should be afraid; by now you've had
enough experience of life's pitfalls.

Medea: Never has Luck will all its twists and turns
challenged as yet my primacy in power.   520

Jason: Acastus does so now.

Medea: And Creon is
a closer enemy. So run away
from both. Medea is not forcing you
to play at civil war, to take up arms
against your in-laws or bloody your hands
by slaughtering your relatives. You need
harm nobody. Just run away with me.

Jason: And who will stand against them if they pose
a threat of war upon two fronts? What if
Acastus joins his forces with Creon's?

Medea: Throw in the Colchians and Aeetes.
Add Scythians to Greeks. I'll sink them all.

Jason: I fear great power.

Medea: Mind you don't lust for it.

Jason: We've talked too long. Let's cut this short right now.   530
People will start to get suspicious.

Medea: Almighty Jupiter, thunder across
the skies, stretch out your arm, ready your fires
of vengeance, burst the veil of clouds, and shake

this tidy world to its foundations.
As you take aim, don't worry which you hit.
If either of us falls, the guilty die.
Your thunderbolt cannot go wrong.

Jason: Get a grip
on sanity, on calm and rational speech.
If there is something from my in-laws' house,
to solace loneliness, ease banishment
for you, just ask.

Medea: You know my will is strong   540
and that my sole response to all the wealth
of kings is pure contempt. I simply want
my children to be free to come with me
while I am on the run. So, when engulfed
in tears, in deep despair, I'll have soothing
kisses. As for you—
                              Aye, new children,
a steady flow, remain to haunt your steps.

Jason: I admit I wish I could obey,
and grant what you apparently desire.
But I *am* their father, and I *must*
refuse. Even my father-in-law, the king,
could not coerce me to comply with this.
It's more than I could stand. My children are
the reason I live on, the thing that makes
me able to endure the pain of all
my ravaged feelings and emotions.
I would more quickly sacrifice my soul,
my body, life itself.

Medea: (*aside*)   Is this how much
he loves his sons? That's good. Then he is caught.   550
Apparently his armor has a chink.
(*to* JASON)
I'm sure you will allow me to tell them,
as I go away, a few last things

I'd like to have them do, and to give them
a final, warm embrace. Even this much
would give me pleasure. Now my last request,
my parting word.
                              I know that, in my pain,
unsure which way to turn, I blurted out
some cruel words. Don't let them haunt your mind.
I want to leave you with a more profound
memorial of me in my better days.
Let every word uttered in anger be
erased to its last letter.

Jason: I untie
the thread of hatred and I banish it
utterly from my mind.
                              Now I myself
have a request: that you please get control
and guide the passionate seething of your mind
into still waters. Calm soothes misery.

(*Exit* JASON. MEDEA *watches him in disbelief. The* NURSE
enters quietly and comes to her side. MEDEA *at first ignores
her; she turns and holds an inner dialogue with herself, alter-
nating between her "first" and "second" persons.*)

Medea: He's gone. Is *that* it? You just stroll away,   560
erase me, erase everything I've done?
Have I just died inside your memory?
Am I cut out? No, I shall never be
cut out.
                Come on then, summon all your strength,
and all your skills. The blessing of a life
lived criminally is that you don't think
of anything as crime.
                              I hardly have
the latitude to spring a trap because
they're all afraid of me.
                              You must attack

75

along a path no one can think could be
a path from which to fear attack. Be bold!
Undertake whatever lies within
Medea's power, whatever lies beyond.
(*to* NURSE)
You've stayed staunch by me through my ups and downs
    of feelings and of fortunes, my dear nurse.
So help me now with my pathetic plans.
I own a robe, a present from the Skies,
the bright possession of my house and realm,
a fiery mark of love the Sun once gave
to Aeetes, his child. I also have   570
a necklace, flashing bright with woven gold.
And there's a crown whose radiance of gems
dulls even the bright flame of gold itself,
comets the wearer's hair to sunlike glow.
I want my sons to carry these as gifts
to the veiled bride. But my infernal skills
must first contaminate them.

                     Let us pray
to Hecate. Prepare the formulae
for death. Erect altars, then kindle fires.
Let flames scream up within the palace walls.

(MEDEA *and the* NURSE *retire into the palace. The* CHO-
RUS *emerges and chants.*)

Chorus: No force of flame, no gust
            of swelling windstorm,   580
            no torqued javelin
            threatens greater danger
            than a wife deprived of
            her husband's affection:
            seething and hating.

            Not when the south wind
            brings the rains of winter;

not when the Danube
floods in raging torrents,
forbidding bridges
to couple its waters,
wandering unbridled.

Not when the Rhone's flow
drives into the salt sea;
not when, dissolving
under solar brightness,
snowcaps become streams,
ice in strong spring sunlight
melts in the Haemus.   590

Fire has no eyes; and
bellowed up with anger
wants no controls, nor
tolerates containment,
never fears death, but
yearns to rush and meet with
swordpoints advancing.

Spare him, o gods, we
beg you to forgive him,
he who has tamed the
seas, let him live safely.
But the lord of ocean,
second just to heaven,
seethes now he is third.

Phaethon, who dared drive
Sun's eternal horses,   600
forgot the pathway
marked out by his father

---

lord of ocean: Neptune (second in rank among the three great gods, Jupiter, Neptune, and Dis)

until the flames he'd
strewn about the heavens
brought ruin on him.

No one has lost much
following the known road.
Go by the path proved
safe to those before us.
Nature is holy;
do not breach her sacred
order with violence.

Each man who roamed in
that daring ship, the *Argo*,
and, to make oars, robbed
Pelion of its timber,
stripping the shade of
its forbidden forests;
each man who passed through
sea's great drifting mountains,   610
then measured ocean's
surface with his bold strokes
and reached his goal, hawsers
tied on foreign coastline,
hot to steal foreign
gold and then return home,
each earned cold justice
from the ocean's hardships—
extermination.

Tiphys was first; the
Breaker of the Ocean
waived his control of
ship to a raw helmsman.
Far from his homeland,
on a foreign seashore,
his star of life set.
Buried like a pauper,

forlorn he lies with   620
ghosts dank and uncremated.
Aulis, from then on,
recalling him, her lost king,
holds vessels. They stand
in the windless harbor
motionless, grieving.

Orpheus, born of
Italian Muse of singing,
plucking his strings in
skillful modulation,
once charmed to standstill
rivers in their rushing,
silenced the winds—each
songbird ceased her trilling,
came to his side, with
the very trees they'd sung in.
Scattered, dismembered
his poor body rotted
on Thracian farmland;   630
but his head kept swimming
down the grim Hebrus
to the Styx and Hell's pit:
no return this time.

Hercules cut down
the twin sons of North wind,
slew the sea's child whose
shape was ever shifting,
exposed to light death's
cruel realm of darkness,
thus bringing peace on
land and upon water.

Italian Muse: Camena
twins sons of North wind: see Boreas and Calais
sea's child: Periclymenus

Then still alive, he
lay on blazing Oeta,
and gave his limbs to
the vicious fire's cremation—   640
a last resort to
escape his hideous torment
of the twin poisons
of watersnake and centaur,
gift of his dear bride.

The bristling boar cut
Ancaeus down with its blow;
you, Meleager,
impiously slaughtered
your mother's brother,
then, when she was angry,
you died at her hands.
All of them deserved death
like that of Hylas,
great Hercules' young friend,
a tender boy who
paid the price for trespass,
dragged to his death in
springs that nymphs were guarding.
Go, plow the salt seas
safely, all you brave men.   650
But fear fresh fountains.

Idmon, who knew what
was to be beforehand,
died of a snakebite
in Libyan Sahara;
Mopsus, unerring
in prophecies for others,
failed in his own case—
precious loss for his Thebes.

---

watersnake and centaur: see Hydra; Nessus

Yet if he truly
sang about the future,
Thetis' husband
aimlessly will wander,
a refugee, and
Nauplius will plunge in
waters that drown him,
after he's tried to   660
wreck the Argive convoy.
Ajax, the son of
Oileus, when sailing,
will pay, struck by lightning,
the sins of his father.
Admetus' wife will
buy back with her own death
her husband's life. Think!
Pelias who ordered
the Golden Fleece brought
back in this, the first boat,
was seared with skill in-
side a heated cauldron:
a steward wandering
on narrow straits of torment.
Enough, gods, the sea
is avenged now; so spare Jason,
for he had no choice.

Exit CHORUS.

Thetis' husband: Peleus

ACT IV

Enter NURSE.

Nurse:

My soul quivers in terror; a hideous act   670
of savagery impends. Some monstrous thought
has taken root and grows, her anguish fuels
itself and gathers its spent violence.
I've often seen her rage, claw down the sky,
attack its deities; yet now Medea
readies for us some huger spectacle,
huger than these. As if lightning-struck,
reeling, she came out, then plunged into
her inner sanctum where she compounds death,
opening every vial and cabinet,
taking ingredients that even she
had always feared. She set out her evil
potions in chaotic rows: arcane
secrets of her own experiments.
Raising her left hand in prayer before   680
her darkly sacred fire, she calls upon
lethal energy Saharan sand
unleashes and creates with seething heat,
and energy the northern mountains hold
motionless, frozen in Arctic ice—
everything that stuns the eye comes forth.
Lured by the enchantment of her voice,
scaly creatures in chaotic mass
snake from their nests: a savage serpent worms
its monstrous body, poises, flickering
its pitchfork tongue, and wonders who to kill.
As it hears her song, it stiffens, twines
its swollen length, forced into heaps of coils.   690

But Medea says: "The evils earth
creates below, within its deepest shafts
make shafts too paltry for my use. I'll seek
poisons from the skies; for it is time
to conjure something loftier, beyond
mere common magic tricks and sleight of hand.

I want the Dragon from the sky, whose coils
are so immense that heaven's two stellar Bears
feel its effect. Phoenicians guide their ships
by the Lesser of these Bears; the Greeks
sail by the Greater.
              Then, let Hercules
relax his grip upon the snake he holds
so that its viral venom spurts.
                  Then let
the Python respond to my song, a snake   700
who dared attack Diana and her twin.

I want the Hydra back. Its every head,
cut off by Hercules, must be restored.
For it renews its life by being cut.

Guardian dragon of Colchis, you come too,
lulled to your first sleep by these songs of mine."

Everything snakelike now evoked, she then
prepares her fruits of evil, heaping them
into a pile: all that the wilderness
near Eryx grows; produce of Caucasus,
those ridges smothered in endless winter,
splattered with Prometheus' blood.
The fighting Mede, the flighty Parthian,   710
the wealthy Arab: she employs toxins
into which they dip their arrowheads.
She uses juices Suebian ladies seek
amid the dankness of their black forests
under an ice-cold sky.

Her hand harvests
whatever earth creates in nesting spring
or when brittle frost balds trees' beauty,
forcing life inside itself with cold:
grasses virulent with deadly flowers,
harmful juices squeezed from twisted roots.

Mount Athos brought her those particular herbs.   720
These came from massive Pindus. That she cut
on a high ridge of Pangaeus; when it lost
its tender, hairlike crown, it left traces
of blood upon the sickle blade.
                                        Now these
grew by the Tigris at low-water time;
those by the Danube, these, by Hydaspes
whose warm streams bear rubies through arid plains;
these by Spanish Baetis—hence the name
Baetica—which languidly lashes
the western ocean at its estuary.

These felt the steel while Phoebus readied day.
That shoot? Cut down at dead of night. And this?
Snipped by her consecrated fingernail.   730

She harvests deadly grasses, milks the snakes'
venom, mixes in birds that bode death:
heart of the mournful horned owl, and the guts
of raucous screech-owl cut out while the bird
was still alive.
                        My mistress of black arts
keeps some ingredients separate. In them
there is the tearing violence of fire.
In others, the icy chill of cramping cold.
Then to her venoms she adds words equal
in terror. Hear the sounds made by her mad
steps and songs at whose first utterance
the ordered universe shudders. Look!

Medea: Silent hordes and gods of death, I call upon you all in
        prayer: 740
Chaos—unseeing and unseen abyss—dark home of
      ghostly Dis,
caverns of decomposing Death, dungeoned by Tartarus'
      steep slopes,
tormented souls, take respite, run and see this novel
      wedding night.
The limb-wrenching wheel must stop, and Ixion must
      touch the ground;
Tantalus must slake his thirst at Corinth, fearing no
      deceit;
one exception: Sisyphus, forebear of Jason's new in-
      laws—
increase his torment, let the slipping stone roll him
      across the crags.
You Danaids whose leaking urns mock your attempts to
      fill them up,
come, be fulfilled together. This day needs your hus-
      band-killing hands.

Hecate, star of night, I call you to my ritual. Come
      now,   750
you have three faces you can threaten vengeance with;
      put on your worst.

For you my hair falls down, unribboned, free,
as is traditional among my race.
With bare feet I have crossed the hidden grove,
enacting lasting rites, drawn water forth
from dry veils of cloud and forced the sea
down to its depths, I have outdone the tides;
Ocean has sucked his massive waters deep
into himself. Laws of astrology
break down: the universe sees sun and stars
together, and the Great and Lesser Bears
dip in forbidden moisture of the sea.
I have bent the laws that govern time:

my spells make spring flowers bloom in summer
    heat;   760
I force the goddess of the grain to watch
turf turned to fruit and crops in winter's cold.
Back to its springs raging Rioni turns;
the Danube idles all its many mouths,
squeezes its surging floods within its banks.
Waves roar, the mad sea swells although the winds
are muted. Rooflike shade provided by
a sacred, ancient wood is gone: sunlight,
at my command, has been brought back again.
Bright Phoebus halts at his zenith. Down slip
the rainy Hyades, moved by my spells.
Time now, dark Phoebe, for your sacred rites.   770

For you: these wreaths I wove with bloodstained hand
    with nine snakes intertwined.
For you: these limbs from rebel Typhoeus who
    shook Jupiter's control.
This, treacherous Nessus' dying blood. He swore
    safe passage over streams.
These, ashes from Oeta's dying fire, which drank
    Hercules' poisoned manhood.
Here, Althaea's brand of vengeance: holy sister
    but unholy mother.   780
These plumes the Harpy left in pathless lair
    when fleeing North wind's son.
Add feathers of Stymphalian bird, shot down
    by Hydra-poisoned arrows.
Altars, you cry aloud: I see my cauldrons
    stirred by god's consent.

I see the witching moon moving in swift arc
yet not driving with her full face shining
night long. Like torchlight, lurid in a graveyard,
she glows as when magicians' spells torment her.   790
Reins taut, she holds course, hugging the horizon.

Moon, now your fire has hues of deathly pallor,
pour waves of grim light on the winds to frighten
mankind. Give people something new to awe them.
Corinthians can pound upon their precious bronzes
to ward off spells.
     On grass red with bloodstains,
I offer to you beasts ritually butchered.
For you a fire-torch snatched from a cremation
burns in the night; for you I arch and toss back 800
my head, I sing, I loose my hair, then bind it
with sacred headband, as they do at funerals.
For you I grip this bough shriveled with death's dew.
For you I bare my breast, slice into my arms
with holy knife, shed my sanity and blood.

Let blood on handsome altars; let hands alter
habits, steel themselves, turn caring to carnage.
(MEDEA *slashes her arms with a sacrificial knife, and lets her*
blood drip on the altar.)
I strike. The stream flows. I have given it. 810

Do you complain, Hecate, child of Perses,
that in my prayers I summon you too often?
However often I summon you the cause is
ever one and the same: his name is Jason.
(*She takes out the robes which are to be her present to Creusa*
and sprinkles them with poisonous liquid.)
Tincture the robes I present to Creusa.
Flame, snake, and sear your way into her bones
the very instant that she puts them on.
(*She packs the robes in a box made of gold.*)
Locked in this yellow womb of gold lurks fire. 820
She'll never fear its presence. Prometheus,
who concealed stolen celestial flames,
gave it to me. He taught me to conceal
its power with art. He paid the penalty:
the life that grew in him.

87

                              Vulcan gave me
fire hidden in powdery sulphur.
Phaethon, like me, kindled from fire, supplied
bolts of living flame. And I have gifts
from medial parts of dragon Chimaera,
flames ripped from seared throat of fire-breathing bull,
mixed with Medusa's gall. These I control;   830
they work my evil will in total silence.

Hecate, stiffen my poison's potency,
and keep its seminal fire deep buried in
my gifts. They must deceive the eye and trick
the touch. The heat must surge into her breast,
come into veins, her limbs must melt,
her bones must smoke, the new bride's hair must burn
outshining the torches of her wedding night.

My prayer is granted. Hecate boldly   840
bays approval, proclaims it with
gleaming torch of blessed fire.

My energy has done what it must do.
Summon my sons to bear these priceless gifts
to the veiled bride.
(*Enter* MEDEA'S SONS, *who take the gifts.*)
                              Go, go my sons,
brood of a cursed mother, and appease
your stepmother, mistress of your fate,
with this offering and many a prayer.
Be off! But hurry home so I can have
the pleasure of a farewell kiss from you.

(*Exeunt* MEDEA *and her* SONS; *enter* CHORUS.)

Chorus: Already she is bloodied;
             savage love ravishes   850
             sanity, sends her reeling.
             But does her rage have power

to shape itself to action?
Vengeance burns in her face,
quickened, then set with anger.
Proudly tossing her head,
beastlike, this mere exile,
makes threats on a king.
It is beyond believing.

Her cheeks flare red. Then cloaking
fear routs red with whiteness—
wild shifts of shape and color.   860
So, when her children perish,
a tigress roams through Ganges'
jungle: mad, obsessed with
ritual, futile searching.

Medea does not know how to
rein in love or anger.
Now love and anger couple
in common cause. What follows?
Will this heathen Colchian
never take her madness
from Greek lands, dissolving,   870
as she sails, fear's grip on
realms and reigning monarchs?
Phoebus, run your course now
with no reins to hold you.
Let kind night bury sunlight,
and evening star that brings night
drown daytime deep in Ocean.

ACT V

Enter MESSENGER, *approaching* MEDEA's *house.*

Messenger: Death is everywhere. Whatever stood
within this royal house has fallen now: 880
father and daughter dead, their ashes mixed.

Chorus: How were they trapped?

Messenger: The way all kings are trapped:
by gifts.

Chorus: What treachery could have been there?

Messenger: I am amazed, hardly believe myself
the evil that is done could have been done.

Chorus: Is there no limit to catastrophe?

Messenger: Fire rages greedily through every part
of the king's residence. It's now destroyed,
completely. The city'll burn next we fear.

Chorus: Use water on the flames to put them out.

Messenger: That's what is so unnerving in this blaze:
water fuels the flames. Uncannily,
the fire burns fiercer when we damp it down.
It overwhelms our one line of defense.   890

(MEDEA *and the* NURSE *enter during this interchange, just
before the* MESSENGER's *last words. Exit* MESSENGER *at the
end of his last speech.*)

Nurse: Quick, leave this land where kings kill sons.
              Hurry, Medea, to any land you want.

Medea: I withdraw? Even if I'd run away
              before, this I'd return to see: marriage
              in a new style.
                           And yet you *do* withdraw,
my soul. Why? Your attack has just paid off.
Follow it up! You take delight in such
a tiny fraction of your vengeance.
If it's enough for you, demented mind,
that Jason not remarry, then you still
love him. Try to find some novel way
to penalize him, and prepare yourself.
Your sense of sin, of shame must be expelled;   900
it is what must get out, withdraw, not you.
If the hand that punishes is clean,
its vengeance is impugned. So put your back
into your anger, wake up from your sleep.
Aggression, which has penetrated deep,
lurks at the bottom of your heart. Suction
it out, be violent, let everything
you've done till now be called an act of love.
Move, and make them learn how trivial
and like a petty criminal's have been
the past crimes I devised. With them my pain
just flexed its strength. What power have untrained arms
to dare great deeds? The bloodlust of a girl!
Now I'm indeed Medea. My genius
has grown with all these evils I have done.   910
I'm pleased I killed my brother, took his head,
and sliced his limbs. I'm glad I tore away
my father's secret source of potency,
I'm glad I armed old Pelias' daughters,
had him killed.
                   You feel the pain, so find
something to exorcise it on. Your hand
is trained for any deed that you must do.

Anger, you must find a way. Our foe
has broken his agreement. So what shafts
do you have poised to hurl?
                My mind within
increasingly decrees atrocity
of some sort; but as yet it lacks courage
to describe it to itself.
              Fool!
I've moved too soon. I should have waited till
my foe had fathered children on his whore.   920

But anything that's yours and came from him
Creusa brought to birth.
                In fancy, then,
it pleases me to penalize him thus
as he deserves. It pleases me. My mind
must be readied for the ultimate crime,
I recognize this now. Children, once mine,
you pay the penalty for father's crimes.

My heart has missed a beat, my limbs are cold.
I feel a shiver in my breast. Anger
has gone, the wife in me has been expelled,
the mother has returned. How can I shed
the blood of my children, my own flesh?
Anger and madness must not come to this!   930
This is a hideous and unnatural act.
I do not understand it. Far be it
from me! What crime would they be paying for,
poor lads? That Jason is their father—or
worse, that I, Medea, am their mother?

They must die, they are not mine. They're mine,
so they are doomed.
              But they are innocent.
they've done no crime, they're guilty of no sin.
That troubles me—and yet my brother, he
was harmless too.

　　　　　Mind, you vacillate
so much. Why do tears dampen your face,
why does anger tear you one way now
and love another? Passion's fierce swell
controls me but cannot decide which way
to toss me. It is as if I were the sea:
violent winds wage war, waves full of grief　　　　940
that rends the heart attack from either side,
the waters seethe in indecision. That
is how my heart wavers. Anger routs love
then love routs anger.
　　　　　　　Pain, yield to love.

Flesh of my flesh, come here. For only you
have shared my loneliness, my ruined home.
Bring yourselves here and drape your limbs round me;
snuggle you little couple. Your father
can have you safe and sound provided your
mother can have you too.
　　　　　　　But exile looms,
and I'll be on the run. They'll soon, too soon,
be torn from my embrace, weeping, groaning
as they kiss me. To their mother they are
forever gone and lost, so they must be
gone and lost to their father as well.　　　　950
My pain grows once again, my hatred boils,
the old avenging fury reaches out
for my unwilling yet so lethal hand.
Anger, I follow your lead. I wish my womb,
like proud Niobe's, had produced a riot
of children, oh, I wish I'd given life
to twice her seven sons. I am as good
as childless now it comes to penalizing
him. I bore only two; but they're enough
to avenge my brother and father.

A riot of furies, overpowering,
is moving in. Where? Who are they hunting?

93

Who will they strike with brandished, searing lash?
This army from the pit of hell waves torches
blazing with blood. At whom? A huge snake snaps   960
loudly like a whip. Who is Megaera
pursuing with firebrand of doom?

                          A ghost
appears, I can't see whose, all dismembered:
It is my brother, come to punish me.

We'll pay the penalty, all of us will pay!
Fix blazing torches where my eyes now shine,
then rip and sear my breast; see now, my heart
lies open for the Furies to enter.

Brother, go from me now and tell the dead
and the avenging goddesses they can
cut back beneath the earth without a care.
Leave me to myself, I'll handle this.
See, brother, I have drawn my sword for you.
(*drawing out a knife and pulling back one* SON*'s head*)
My hand's deed placates my brother dead.   970
(MEDEA *kills the* CHILD *but is then distracted by a sudden
noise of people approaching from offstage.*)
A sudden sound. What does it mean? Weapons!
They're taking up arms to kill me.

                         Then I'll climb
onto the very rooftop of my house.
The slaughter's just half done.
(*to her living* CHILD)

                      You, come with me,
and keep me company.
(*to her dead* CHILD)

                  I'll also take
your body with me as I leave.

                         Mind,
concentrate and face things like a man.
Don't hide your deed. The people will applaud.

(MEDEA *climbs up to the rooftop as* JASON, *accompanied by a crowd of* CORINTHIANS, *enters and speaks.*)

Jason: If you are loyal and feel sorrow and pain
at the calamity that strikes your kings,
then join me quickly, and we will arrest
the perpetrator of this hideous crime.   980
This way, men-at-arms, and bring your spears.
Turn this house over from top to bottom.

Medea: Now I have you back again: my power,
my brother, and my father. Now Colchis
has regained its stolen fleece of gold.
My kingdom has come back to me again;
now my rape, my motherhood, are gone
and my virginity returns. At last,
powers of nature, you have been appeased.
This is a real wedding-day of joy.
The crime is now complete, so go. But no:
I am not yet avenged.
                    Then finish it
while your hands can act. Don't fail me now,
dear mind, don't delay, you have the power.
Your anger has already dropped. You now   990
regret what you have done. You are ashamed.

Pathetic woman, what have you done—
what have *I* done? Pathetic? Sorry I am,
but I have done it. And against my will
a sense of pleasure subtly penetrates
my being, and it grows, constantly grows.
It lacked only one thing to be perfect.
He should have seen it. So I have achieved
nothing as yet. For any criminal act
is just a waste without him here to see.

Jason: Look! There she stands. See, where the roof slopes
    down,

      threatening. Bring torches, one of you,
      then let her fall, scorched by her own fires.

Medea: Gather wood to build your sons a fire,
      build them a tomb, Jason. Your new father
      and wife have all the rites the dead should have.
      I saw to their cremation. This one son
      has met his doom. Now you are here to watch,   1000
      the other will be given a matching death.

Jason: By every power of nature, by ordeals
      we suffered through together on the run,
      by my sexual fidelity
      to you, which I never betrayed, I beg you,
      spare our son. If there is any crime,
      it's mine; I yield! The guilt is on my head!
      So kill me, and make me your sacrifice!

Medea: Here, where you beg me not to, I shall drive
      the steel; here, where it gives you pain. So go,
      proud hero, hunt down virgins in their rooms,
      leave them when they are mothers.

Jason: One is enough
      to penalize me.

Medea: If the slaughtering
      of only one could satisfy my hand,
      I would have killed no one at all. And two
      are trivial repayment for my pain,   1010
      If, even now, there is, unknown to me,
      some fetus spawned by you inside my womb,
      I'll use this sword and tear it out with steel.

Jason: You've started your great deed. So finish it.
      That was my final prayer for mercy. This
      is now the favor that I ask: do not
      delay my punishment.

Medea: Enjoy your crime,
my aching heart, enjoy it to the full.
The day is mine; I urge you not to hurry.
We are using the time that we were given.

Jason: Damned woman, kill me.

Medea: Pity is your demand.
I pity you. It's done.
(MEDEA *kills the other child*.)
                    I had no more
to offer, aching heart, in recompense.
Jason, lift up your swollen eyes to me.   1020
Ungrateful Jason, do you now know your wife?
This is my sole, inevitable way
of going into exile. A pathway
into the hidden sky that my paternal
ancestry reveals has opened up.
Twin serpents offer me their scaly necks
to bridge me to the stars. Obey, dear parent,
take your children back, and I shall ride
in winged course upon the breath of winds.

Jason: Wade through the deep expanses of boundless,
shining sky. Wherever you may go,
you'll prove the nonexistence of all gods.

Glossary

The brief summaries given here are based on the Senecan versions of the myths. Other ancient writers often give different accounts. Variants are mentioned only where necessary for clarity. An asterisk next to a name indicates that it has its own entry elsewhere in the glossary. The Latin names are used except when an accepted English version exists.

Absyrtus   Son of Aeetes* and brother of Medea;* killed by Medea, who then threw his limbs into the sea as she fled from Colchis.*

Acastus   King of Iolcus,* in Thessaly;* son of Pelias,* Jason's* uncle and enemy.

Achaean   Greek.

Acharnia   An area in Attica* north of Athens.

Acheron   One of four frequently mentioned rivers of the Greek underworld.

Achilles   Son of the goddess Thetis* and her mortal husband, Peleus,* born in Phthia* in Thessaly;* educated by the centaur Chiron.* At the outbreak of the Trojan War, Thetis disguised him as a girl (to keep him from being drafted into the army) and kept him on the island of Scyros,* where he raped a girl named Deidamia, thus fathering Pyrrhus.* Eventually he betrayed himself to the Greek military recruiters, led by Ulysses,* by his fascination with the weapons they brought.

Acte   Another name for Attica.*

Admetus   Mythical king of Thessaly* whose wife, Alcestis,* died in his place but was brought back from the dead by Hercules.*

Aeacus   Father of Peleus;* grandfather of Achilles;* frequently thought of as a ruler among the dead.

Aeetes   King of Colchis;* father of Medea* and Absyrtus.*

Aegaleus   A mountain range in Attica.*

Aegeus   Father of Theseus.★ The Aegean Sea was named for him. See
    Sunion.
Aeolus   Father of Sisyphus;★ ancestor of Creon★ of Corinth★ and his daugh-
    ter Creusa.★
Aeson   Father of Jason;★ king of Iolcus,★ deposed by Pelias.★
Aetna   A volcano in Sicily; mythical abode of Vulcan,★ god of fire.
Agamemnon   King of Mycenae;★ son of Atreus,★ brother of Menelaus.★
    Leader of the Greek expedition against Troy,★ he sacrificed his own
    daughter to obtain favorable winds (see Aulis). His quarrel with
    Achilles,★ who objected to Agamemnon's seizure of his concubine
    Briseis,★ is a major motif of Homer's *Iliad*.
Ajax   (1) The "Greater" Ajax, son of Telamon, was the best of the Greek
    warriors at Troy★ after Achilles;★ he committed suicide when the
    dead Achilles' armor was awarded to Ulysses★ rather than to him.
    (2) The "Lesser" Ajax, son of Oileus,★ was shipwrecked on his
    return from the Trojan War.
Alcestis   Wife of Admetus.★ She was brought back to life by Hercules★
    after she died in her husband's place.
Alcides   A descendant of Alc(a)eus, the father of Amphitryon; always =
    Hercules★ in Seneca.
Alcmena   Wife of Amphitryon. Seduced by Jupiter,★ who disguised himself
    as her husband, she gave birth to Hercules.★
Alpheus   A river in the Peloponnesus.
Althaea   Mother of Meleager,★ whose life, she was told at his birth, could
    last only as long as a certain log burning in the fire. She immediately
    seized the log from the flames, but years later, when Meleager killed
    her beloved brothers, in anger she threw it back into a fire. As
    predicted, Meleager died when the log was consumed.
Amazons   A group of nomadic, man-hating female warriors whose home-
    land is usually given as the region around the Black Sea: Maeotis,★
    Thermodon,★ Pontus.★ The Greeks had several mythical battles
    with them. Theseus★ fought them and forced Antiope★ to become
    his wife; she bore him a son, Hippolytus,★ but Theseus later put
    her to death. Penthesilea★ led a band of Amazons against the Greeks
    at Troy and was killed by Achilles.★
Amor   Cupid;★ especially popular among the Roman poets because his
    name spelled backward is Roma. In Vergil's *Aeneid* and elsewhere
    in Latin literature, Aeneas, founder of the Roman race, is Amor's
    brother.
Amyclae   A city near Sparta;★ Sparta's "twin city." Its name is often used
    to indicate Sparta itself.
Ancaeus   An Argonaut from Tegea, in the Peloponnesus, who replaced
    Tiphys★ as helmsman of the *Argo*★ after Tiphys' death.
Andromache   Daughter of Eetion;★ wife of Hector;★ mother of Astyanax.★

She was taken from Troy★ by Pyrrhus★ after the city's fall and was ultimately married to Hector's brother, Helenus.★

Antenor   A Trojan warrior; husband of Theano, priestess of the goddess Minerva (Pallas)★ at Troy.★ In some traditions Antenor and Aeneas, son of Venus,★ betrayed Troy to the Greeks.

Antiope   A queen of the Amazons.★ She appears in three distinct traditions: (1) as a wife of Theseus★ (see Amazons); (2) as the queen whose girdle Hercules★ must win as his ninth labor; (3) as mother of Amphion and Zethus, the builders of Thebes'★ walls.

Aonia   Thebes.★

Aphidnae   An area of Attica★ near Marathon.★

Apollo   See Phoebus.

Aquilo   See Boreas.

Araxes   An Armenian river, today the Aras; often a symbol to Roman writers of the eastern boundary of Roman power.

Arcadia   A mountainous and primitive part of Greece whose inhabitants were supposedly the earliest inhabitants of Greece; they are often depicted as people of either ideal simplicity or primitive barbarism. Roman tradition maintained that the first settlement of the site of Rome was made by an exiled king of Arcadia, Evander, a descendant of Lycaon,★ "Wolfman."

Arctus   The constellation Ursa Major (the Great Bear or Big Dipper), the main constellation used by the Greeks for navigation. The Phoenicians and Carthaginians sailed by the Lesser Bear (Ursa Minor), known as Cynosura. In myth the Great Bear is Callisto,★ daughter of Lycaon.★ After her rape by Jupiter★ she was turned into a bear by Diana,★ then saved from hunters by Jupiter,★ who placed her in the skies.

Argo   The ship that conveyed Jason★ and the Argonauts (i.e., "sailors in *Argo*") to and from Colchis;★ in some traditions, the first ship ever made. *Argo*'s keel was made of oak from the prophetic shrine of Dodona; the vessel itself could speak.

Argos   A major city in the Peloponnesus, often not distinguished from Mycenae.★ The adjective "Argive" is often used to mean "Greek."

Ariadne   Daughter of Minos,★ king of Crete, and of Pasiphae,★ his wife; sister of Phaedra★ and the Minotaur.★ She fell in love with Theseus★ and saved him from death in the labyrinth by supplying him with a thread made by Daedalus★ which enabled Theseus to escape from the labyrinth after killing the Minotaur, who was imprisoned there. Theseus took Ariadne with him as he left Crete but abandoned her on the island of Naxos. She was saved by Bacchus,★ who made her his wife and ultimately set her in the heavens as a star.

Assaracus   Great-grandson of Dardanus;★ brother of Jupiter's★ Trojan lover Ganymede; great-grandfather of Aeneas, who was regarded by some Roman writers as founder of the Roman people.

Assyria   Very roughly the equivalent of parts of modern Iraq; to Roman writers it included Syria as well. The area was proverbial for its luxurious living and particularly for its perfumes.

Astyanax   Son of Hector* and Andromache;* killed on instructions from Calchas.*

Athos   A high peninsula jutting out into the Aegean from the Thracian coast.

Atreus   Father of Agamemnon* and Menelaus* (who are collectively known as the Atridae); feuded with his brother Thyestes,* whose children he murdered and served as a meal to their father.

Attica   The section of Greece in which the city of Athens is situated.

Aulis   A coastal city of Euboea, in Greece, from which the Greeks sailed to Troy.* Here, to obtain favorable winds, Agamemnon* sacrificed his daughter Iphigenia at the bidding of the priest Calchas.*

Ausonian   A general poetic term for the non-Greek-speaking ancient inhabitants of Italy.

Auster   The south wind, bringer of clouds and rain.

Avernus   The Italian equivalent of Taenarum;* a lake near Cumae, in the Bay of Naples area, which supposedly welled up from the underworld.

Bacchus   God of wine, proverbially beautiful; also known as Lyaeus, Liber, Bromius, and Dionysus.

Baetis   The river Guadalquivir, in Spain.

Bessa   A small town near Scarphe,* in Locris (central Greece).

Boötes   A constellation near the Greater and Lesser Bears.

Boreas   The north wind, father of Calais* and Zetes.*

Briseis   A woman from Lyrnesos* captured by Achilles* and kept as his lover. She was seized from Achilles by Agamemnon* when Agamemnon was forced to relinquish his own captive lover, Chryseis.*

Bromius   See Bacchus.

Busiris   A mythical Egyptian king who sacrificed at the altar of Jupiter* all foreigners who entered his land.

Calais   Son of Boreas;* twin of Zetes; drove off the Harpies* from their homeland; killed (with Zetes) by Hercules.*

Calchas   A Greek prophet who told Agamemnon* he must sacrifice his own daughter to obtain favorable winds for the voyage to Troy.* He also ordered that Astyanax* and Polyxena* be sacrificed to secure the Greeks' safe return.

Callisto   Daughter of Lycaon.* See Arctus.

Calydnae   Two small islands off the coast of Asia Minor, near Troy.*

Calydon   Town in Aetolia (Greece), most famous in myth for a boar hunt which took place there. It was during this hunt that Meleager* killed his uncles.

Camena   The Latin equivalent of the Greek *Mousa*, Muse. Seneca's choice of this word to indicate the mother of the Greek bard Orpheus★ is striking, as Roman poets tended to use *Musa* rather than *Camena* in reference to Greek poetic muses. Compare his use of the Latin term *fescennine*.★

Carystos   A city at the south end of the island of Euboea (Greece).

Cassandra   Daughter of Priam★ and Hecuba;★ priestess of Phoebus.★ She agreed to become the god's lover in return for the gift of prophecy but finally refused to have sex with him. Phoebus punished her by decreeing that no one would believe her prophecies. After the fall of Troy★ she was assigned to Agamemnon★ as his prize.

Castor   Brother of Pollux;★ one of *Argo*'s crew. The two brothers, who spent half of each year alive and half dead, were known and worshiped together as the divine Dioscuri ("Boys of Zeus," in Greek) and were believed to protect sailors. Castor was famous for his horsemansip and his horse Cyllarus; Pollux was famous for his boxing.

Caucasus   A mountain or mountainous area near the Caspian Sea; the mythical site where Prometheus★ was kept in chains.

Caycus   The principal river of Mysia★ (Turkey).

Cecrops   A mythical forebear of the Athenian people, half man, half snake. The adjective "Cecropian" is often used as a general equivalent of "Athenian."

Cephallenia   An Ionian★ island southwest of Ithaca; the name is often used to indicate Ithaca.

Cerberus   A mythical three-headed dog who guarded the entrance/exit of the underworld.

Ceres   Mother Earth; goddess of crops.

Chalcis   A powerful city of Euboea (Greece), one of whose colonies was Cumae, in Italy.

Charybdis   A dangerous mythical whirlpool in the sea, facing Scylla.★

Chimaera   A mythical monster, part goat, part lion, part snake.

Chiron   A centaur (half horse, half man) associated with Mount Pelion,★ in Thessaly;★ tutor of Achilles.★ Although immortal, he was wounded by Hercules★ with a poisoned arrow, and in his pain begged to be allowed to die.

Chryse   A small town near Troy.★

Chryseis   Daughter of Chryses, a priest of Phoebus;★ taken as a concubine by Agamemnon★ but released when Phoebus sent a plague upon the Greek army. Agamemnon took Briseis★ from Achilles★ as a replacement for Chryseis.

Cicero   A Roman orator of the first century B.C. In his first oration against Catiline (a Roman noble who Cicero believed was plotting to overthrow the government), Cicero appealed to Catiline to "free the citizens from fear" by leaving Rome. Seneca's Creon★ echoes these words in *Medea*.

Cilla   A small town near Chryse.★

Cnossos   The principal city of ancient Crete; home of Minos,★ Phaedra,★ and the Minotaur.

Colchis   Medea's★ hometown, on the eastern shore of the Black Sea (now in the Soviet Union).

Corinth   A city on the isthmus connecting the Peloponnesus to northern Greece.

Corus   The northwest wind.

Cossack   = Scythian★ in these translations.

Creon   King of Corinth;★ father of Creusa.★

Creusa   Daughter of Creon.★

Cupid   God of love = Amor,★ often represented by Romans as the son of Venus.★

Cybele   The earth-mother goddess (also known as Cybebe), whose cult was centered on Mount Ida,★ near Troy,★ Her cult was also well established in Rome.

Cyclades   Islands in the Aegean.

Cygnus   The invulnerable son of Neptune,★ whom Achilles★ killed by strangulation; Neptune metamorphosed him into a swan.

Cyllarus   The special horse of Castor.★

Daedalus   An Athenian craftsman, who helped the Cretan queen Pasiphae★ consummate her love for a white bull by making her a cowsuit of wood. Pasiphae's child by this mating, the Minotaur, was imprisoned within a maze (labyrinth) designed by Daedalus at the request of Pasiphae's husband, Minos.★ After Daedalus helped the lovesick Ariadne★ save Theseus★ from death in the labyrinth—he gave her a ball of thread that enabled Theseus to retrace his steps—Minos imprisoned him (in, according to some accounts, his own artistic marvel, the labyrinth). Daedalus escaped with his son, Icarus, by creating wings of feathers and wax, but Icarus fell to earth and died because he flew too close to the sun, which melted the wax of his wings.

Danaans   The people of Danaus★ (king of Argos★); the Greeks.

Danaids   The fifty daughters of Danaus,★ king of Argos,★ who, with one exception, killed their husbands, the sons of Aegyptus, king of Egypt.

Danaus   King of Argos.★

Dardanus   Ancestor of the people of Troy;★ son of Teucer★ or of Jupiter.★ In some traditions, Dardanus arrived in Troy from Italy.

Deucalion   The Greek Noah; one of two survivors of the Great Flood sent by Jupiter★ to punish sinful mortals. See Pyrrha.

Diana   Sister of Phoebus,★ also called Phoebe;★ goddess of the moon and of magic; often indistinguishable from Hecate.★

Dictynna   A Cretan goddess, identified with Diana.★

Diomedes (1) A companion of Ulysses.★ In a famous night expedition at
  Troy,★ the two killed a Trojan spy, Dolon, and a newly arrived
  Trojan ally, Rhesus,★ and his men. They then made off with Rhesus' wonderful horses. (2) A mythical king of Thrace★ who fed
  human flesh to his horses until Hercules★ took the horses away
  from him.

Dis God of (buried) wealth; god of the dead = Pluto.★

dryads Female tree spirits (nymphs) often pursued by (or in pursuit of) the
  god Pan.★

Eetion Father of Andromache;★ killed, along with his seven sons, by
  Achilles.★

Eleusis A city in Attica,★ famous as the site of the rites of the goddess
  Ceres★ (Greek Demeter).

Elysium The (underworld) home of the blessed dead.

Endymion A handsome youth with whom the Moon (Diana)★ fell in love,
  and who, in many versions of the myth, sleeps eternally.

Enispe A small town in Arcadia★ (Greece).

Epidauros A coastal town not far from Argos★ (Greece), famous for its
  temple of Aesculapius, the god of healing and medicine.

Erebus The darkness of death and the underworld; the underworld itself.

Erinys The goddess of vendettas, who avenges bloodguilt; often named
  either Megaera★ or Tisiphone.

Eryx Son of Venus★ and Hercules,★ in whose honor a mountain in Sicily
  (famous for its temple of Venus) was named.

Europa Daughter of Agenor, a king of Phoenicia (ancient Lebanon); sister
  of Cadmus, founder of Thebes★ (Greece); abducted by Jupiter★
  disguised as a bull; mother of Minos,★ king of Crete.

Fate That which is spoken or decreed; destiny, fate.

Fescennine A ribald, farcical Italian song, sung at Roman weddings; one
  of the specifically Italian elements in Seneca's representation of Jason's★ wedding. See Camena.

Fortune An Italian goddess, (temperamental) bringer of produce and good
  luck.

Furies Vengeful spirits of the dead. See Erinys.

Gaetulians People of North Africa (Tunis and Morocco).

Garamantians People of Saharan Africa.

Getae Nomadic and barbaric Thracian (Balkan) people.

Gonoessa A small town near Sicyon, in the Peloponnesus (Greece).

Gradivus The stepping, marching god: Mars.★

Greater Bear See Arctus.

Gyrton Town in Thessaly★ (Greece).

Haemus A great Balkan mountain range.

Harpies Monstrous creatures, part bird, part woman, chased from their
  home by the twin sons of Boreas.★ See Calais;★ Zetes.

Hebrus A Thracian river (modern Maritza) which flows into the Aegean.

Hecate Goddess of moon, magic, and witchcraft, also of crossroads; often called Trivia, "three-way path." See Diana.

Hector Chief Trojan warrior in the war at Troy;* son of Priam;* husband of Andromache;* killed by Achilles.* Hector's body was ransomed from the Greeks by Priam.

Hecuba Wife of Priam;* mother of Hector,* Cassandra,* Polyxena,* Paris,* and Helenus.*

Helen Daughter of Jupiter* (or Tyndareus)* and Leda; wife of Menelaus,* king of Sparta;* awarded by Venus* as a prize to Paris* (son of Priam,* who took her away to Troy* (see Ida). Her abduction triggered the Trojan War. After Paris' death she was married to his brother Deiphobus.

Helenus Twin brother of Cassandra* and, like her, a prophet; one of the few male survivors of Trojan royal blood; subsequently became king of Buthrotum, in Epirus.

Helle Daughter of Athamas and Nephele. Her mother saved her from being sacrificed and sent her and her brother Phrixus* out to sea on the back of a sheep with a fleece of gold. Helle drowned in the Hellespont (named for her), but Phrixus traveled on to Colchis,* where the sheep was sacrificed and became the Golden Fleece, the object of Jason's* and the Argonauts' quest.

Hercules Son of Jupiter* and Alcmena.* He sailed on the *Argo** but was left behind when his friend Hylas* failed to return to the ship and Hercules stayed ashore too long searching for him. He was the strongest of Greek heroes; his bow, inherited by Philoctetes, was supposedly the critical weapon in the final struggle for Troy.* Among his other labors, he killed the many-headed water snake, the Hydra,* whose poison Medea* wanted. His prowess at killing snakes first manifested itself when, as a child still in his cradle, he strangled two snakes that Juno* had sent to kill him. Yet this masculine hero dressed as a maid when in love with Omphale.

Hercynian Forest A vast forestland in ancient central Europe.

Hermione Daughter of Helen* and Menelaus;* married to Pyrrhus,* who was murdered by Orestes;* finally married Orestes.

Hesperus The evening star; the west.

Hippolytus Son of Theseus* and the Amazon* Antiope.*

Hister The river Danube.

Hyades (1) Daughters of Atlas. (2) The Zodiacal constellation Hyades ("Rainers").

Hydaspes A tributary of the Indus River.

Hydra A many-headed snake killed by Hercules* at Lerna.*

Hylas See Hercules.

Hymen (1) God of (marriage) feasts. (2) A song (hymn) sung at weddings.

Hymettus   The most southerly of the three major mountains in Attica,★ famous for its honey.

Hyrcanians   People who lived near the Caspian Sea.

Ida   A well-timbered mountain near Troy;★ the site of the beauty contest among the goddesses Pallas★ (Minerva), Venus,★ and Juno★ at which Paris★ awarded the prize to Venus★ because she promised to give him Helen★ as his wife.

Idmon   A prophet, one of the Argonauts.

Ilisos   A river in Attica.★

Ilium   Another name for Troy,★ derived from Ilus, the son of Tros (for whom Troy was named).

Iolcos   A city of Thessaly★ (Greece), modern Volos; home of Jason;★ port of departure for the *Argo*.★

Ionian   Asiatic or Athenian Greek, as opposed to mainland and particularly Peloponnesian (Mycenaean) Greek.

Isthmos   See Corinth.

Ithaca   An island in the Ionian Sea; home of Ulysses.★

Ixion   A mythical criminal who attempted to rape Juno★ but was tricked into making love to a phantom made of clouds instead. The offspring of this union were the centaurs. Ixion's son, Pirithous,★ attempted to rape Proserpina,★ wife of Dis★ and goddess of the dead.

Jason   Son of Aeson;★ husband of Medea;★ commander of the *Argo*.★

Juno   Wife and sister of Jupiter;★ patron of Argos★ and of Jason.★

Jupiter   Most powerful of the gods; lord of the thunderbolt; ancestor of the Cretan house of Minos.★

Laertes   Father of Ulysses.★

Laomedon   Father of Priam;★ cheated Neptune★ and Phoebus★ of their wages for building Troy;★ also cheated Hercules★ of his promised reward for saving Laomedon's daughter; as a consequence, Hercules attacked and captured Troy.

Lerna   (1) Home of the Hydra.★ (2) Fountain near Corinth.★

Lesbos   An Aegean island plundered by Achilles★ before the Trojan War.

Lesser Bear   See Arctus.

Lethe   The river of forgetting; one of the rivers of the underworld.

Leucate   An island in the Ionian Sea.

Libra   The zodiacal sign Libra.

Libya   General term for North Africa.

Lucifer   The "Bringer of Light," the morning star.

Lucina   The "Bringer to Light," goddess of childbirth.

Lycaon   "Wolfman." Arcadian king, father of Callisto★; changed into a wolf by Jupiter★ because he killed a human being as a sacrificial offering.

Lynceus   An Argonaut famous for his ability to see great distances.

Lyrnesos   A town in the vicinity of Troy.★

maenad   A woman "possessed" or maddened by the power of a god (usually Bacchus)★ and endowed with superhuman strength and subhuman ferocity.

Maeotis   The Sea of Azov and its environs.

Malea   A headland in the southern Peloponnesus (Greece).

Marathon   A coastal area of eastern Attica;★ home of a fierce bull killed by Theseus.★

Mars   God of war; lover of Venus.★ See Gradivus.

Meander   The Meander (now the Menderes) River, in Asia Minor (Turkey).

Medea   Daughter of Aeetes,★ king of Colchis;★ wife of Jason;★ stepmother of Theseus.★

Medes   Inhabitants of Parthia★ (ancient Iran).

Medusa   A deadly female monster whose hideous face turned anyone who saw her into stone; killed by the hero Perseus.

Megaera   See Erinys.

Meleager   See Althea.

Memnon   Son of Aurora (Dawn), the last ally to come to Troy's★ aid; killed by Achilles★ before the eyes of his mother and his uncle (Priam).★

Menelaus   King of Sparta;★ son of Atreus;★ brother of Agamemnon;★ husband of Helen.★

Minos   King of Crete; father of Phaedra★ and Ariadne.★

Minyae   (1) The people of the Minyius River, in Greece. (2) The Argonauts.

Molossians   People of Epirus famous for their dogs, "Dalmatians."

Mopsopia   Athens.

Mopsus   A prophet; one of the Argonauts.

Mothone   A town at the foot of Mount Pelion,★ in Thessaly★ (Greece); ruled by Philoctetes, whose bow (inherited from Hercules)★ the Greeks needed to procure the fall of Troy.★

Mycenae   A town near Argos;★ home of Agamemnon.★

Mysia   See Telephus.

naiads   Female water spirits (nymphs).

Nauplius   An Argonaut; later lured a Greek fleet to shipwreck because of his anger at the Greeks for their mistreatment of his son Palamedes.

Neptune   God of the (Aegean) sea, of horses, and of earthquakes; father of Theseus★ (Aegeus,★ who is Theseus' father in some versions, is himself essentially "the Aegean"); one of the gods who built Troy.★

Nereids   Female sea deities (nymphs); daughters of Nereus.★

Nereus   A lesser sea god; father of the Nereids★ and of Thetis,★ thus grandfather of Achilles.★

Neritos   An island near Ithaca★ in the Ionian★ Sea.

Nessus   A centaur (see Ixion) who attempted to rape Deianira, a wife of Hercules.★ Hercules killed him with a poisoned arrow, but to gain revenge before he died Nessus gave Deianira some of his poisoned blood, which he said would help her restore Hercules' love if he was ever unfaithful to her. Hercules was unfaithful, and he was given a cloak, tainted with Nessus' blood which caused him to die in agony.

Nestor   The oldest Greek warrior in the Trojan War. His home was Pylos,★ in the western Peloponnesus (Greece).

Niobe   A Theban princess who angered Phoebus★ and Diana★ by boasting that her children were more beautiful than they. As punishment, the two deities shot down all fourteen of Niobe's children with arrows, and she wept until she was turned to stone.

Notos   The southwest wind.

Nysa   A mountain, supposedly in India, associated with Bacchus.★

Oceanus   (1) A mythical river that flows round the world. (2) The Atlantic Ocean.

Oeta   A mountain in Thessaly★ (Greece), where Hercules★ died.

Oileus   An Argonaut; father of one of the two warriors named Ajax★ who fought at Troy.★

Olenus   A Greek town near modern Patras.

Ophiuchus   A constellation, now divided into two: the Snake Holder and the Snake.

Orestes   Son of Agamemnon.★

Orpheus   A Thracian singer, son of the Muse Camena,★ whose songs could beguile even trees and stones to move; an Argonaut. He was killed by maenads★ in Thrace:★ his head was torn off and it floated down the river Hebrus★ into the Aegean and across to Lesbos.★

Pallas   A goddess identified with Minerva (Athena); builder of the *Argo*.★ Pallas' citadel = the acropolis of Athens.

Pan(s)   Goat god(s), pursuers of (and pursued by) dryads.★

Pangaeus Mountain   A mountain in Thrace,★ near Philippi.

Paris   Son of Priam★ and Hecuba;★ abductor of Helen.★ See Ida.

Parnes   A mountain range in Attica.★

Parnethus   An area between Attica★ and Boeotia.

Paros   An Aegean island famous for its marble.

Parthia(ns)   An Iranian people, who became dominant in Persia about 250 B.C.

Pasiphae   Daughter of Sol★ (the Sun); wife of Minos;★ lover of a bull by whom she became mother of the Minotaur (see Daedalus); also mother of Phaedra,★ Ariadne,★ and Androgeos.

Patroclus   A close companion of Achilles★ at Troy.★ When Achilles would not fight because of his quarrel with Agamemnon,★ Patroclus was permitted to put on Achilles' armor and fight in his place. He was thus the "false Achilles." Hector★ killed him.

Pegasus   (1) A horse with wings, born from the blood of the dying gorgon Medusa.★ (2) The constellation Pegasus.

Pelasgians   Aboriginal, non-Greek-speaking inhabitants of Greece.

Peleus   Son of Aeacus,★ often associated with Mount Pelion,★ in Thessaly★
(Greece). Peleus killed his brother Phocus, then traveled to Phthia,★
where he was cleansed of bloodguilt but accidentally killed his
purifier. In exile at Iolcus,★ he was again purified (by Acastus,★
son of Pelias).★ He was rewarded for his courage by being given
Thetis★ as his bride. She bore him Achilles.★

Pelias   Uncle of Jason★ who usurped power at Iolcus★ and sent Jason on
his quest for the Golden Fleece; killed unintentionally by his daughters, who dismembered and cooked him in the mistaken belief that
they could rejuvenate him with Medea's★ spells and potions.

Pelion   A mountain in Thessaly★ (Greece).

Pelops   Son of Tantalus;★ father of Atreus;★ grandfather of Agamemnon★
and Menelaus;★ killed and dismembered by his father to provide a
banquet for Jupiter★ but later restored to life. The Peloponnesus
("Island of Pelops") was thought to be named for him. Thus "Pe-
lopian" often means "Peloponnesian" or "Corinthian," as Corinth★
guards the entrance to the Peloponnesus.

Pelorus   The northeast coast of Sicily, associated with Scylla.★

Penthesilea   Queen of the Amazons★ who led an army against the Greeks
at Troy★ and was killed by Achilles.★

Peparethos   A small island off the coast of Thessaly★ (Greece).

Pergamum   The citadel of Troy.★

Periclymenus   Son of Neptune★ who could change shape; an Argonaut;
killed by Hercules★ while he was in the form of a fly.

Perseis   Wife of Sol★ (the Sun); mother of Aeetes,★ king of Colchis;★ grandmother of Medea.★

Phaedra   Daughter of Minos★ and Pasiphae.★

Phaethon   Son of Sol★ (the Sun). Having persuaded his father to let him
drive the solar chariot for a day, Phaethon lost control of the horses,
caused great damage in heaven and on earth, and was finally struck
by a thunderbolt from Jupiter.★ His body fell into the mythical
river Eridanus. His sisters, who came there to mourn him were
metamorphosed into trees, and their tears became amber.

Pharis   A small town near Sparta★ (Greece).

Phasis   The river Rioni★ (now in the Soviet Union), on which Medea's★
city, Colchis,★ was situated.

Pherae   A city in Thessaly★ (Greece); home of Admetus★ and Alcestis.★

Philoctetes   See Mothone.

Phlegethon   A fiery river of the underworld.

Phlyeis   A region of Attica.★

Phoebe   Goddess of the moon; sister of Phoebus.★ See Diana.

Phoebus   A god famous for his beauty, his bow and arrows, and his love
of music; identified with the daylight and Sol★ (the Sun) and also
called Apollo; one of the gods who built Troy.★

Phrixus   Traveled on the golden-fleeced sheep with his sister Helle.★ Unlike Helle, he arrived safely in Colchis,★ his destination. See Helle.

Phrygia   The area of Asia Minor (Turkey) in which Troy★ was situated.

Phthia   A city in Thessaly★ (Greece) known for the ferocity of its inhabitants, notably Achilles.★

pietas   Dedication to one's gods, country, and family.

Pindus   A high mountain on the borders of Thessaly★ (Greece) and Epirus.

Pirene   A Corinthian fountain from which Tantalus★ drank.

Pirithous   Son of Ixion★ and friend of Theseus.★ He and Theseus went together into the underworld to carry off Proserpina,★ the wife of Dis.★

Pisa   A town in the Peloponnesus (Greece); = Olympia.

Pittheus   King of Troezen,★ in the Peloponnesus; father of Aethra, Theseus'★ mother.

Pleiades   (1) A cluster of stars in the constellation Taurus.★ (2) Daughters of Atlas, the mythical giant who holds up the skies.

Pleuron   A coastal town in Aetolia (Greece).

Pluto   See Dis.

Pollux   See Castor.

Polyxena   Daughter of Priam★ and Hecuba;★ sacrificed on the tomb of Achilles,★ near Troy,★ at the end of the Trojan War.

Pompey   A Roman politican and general of the first century B.C. who symbolized for many Romans the last days of freedom before the domination of the Caesars. He was defeated by Julius Caesar at Pharsalia, in Greece, in 48 B.C. and murdered in Egypt by a soldier named Achillas later in the same year. His body was left headless upon the seashore. Vergil in *Aeneid* 2.557 seems to be alluding to Pompey's death in his description of Priam's★ death, and Seneca seems to be echoing Vergil.

Pontus   The Black Sea area, including the Roman province of Pontus.

Priam   The last king of Troy★ and husband of Hecuba;★ he was twice left at the mercy of the Greeks when Troy was captured: first by Hercules,★ then by Agamemnon.★ Hercules spared his life; Pyrrhus,★ son of Achilles,★ murdered him on an altar. See Pompey.

Procrustes   A highwayman who lived near Eleusis;★ he mutilated and killed travelers by putting them on a short bed and lopping off their extremities if they were tall, or by putting them on a long bed and stretching them if they were small; killed by Theseus.★

Prometheus   A Titan★ who brought Jupiter's★ fire to mortals. For this offense he was chained to a crag on the Caucasus★ Mountain, where an eagle came daily to eat his liver. Each night the liver regrew; each day the eagle returned until Hercules★ killed it.

Proserpina   Daughter of Ceres,★ goddess of crops; abducted by Dis★ to be his wife among the dead. Pirithous★ attempted to carry her off from the underworld with Theseus'★ help.

Proteus   The Old Man of the Sea, a divine or semidivine being who could change into many shapes and was also a prophet. He lived off the coast of Egypt near the site of the famous lighthouse of Pharos, near Alexandria.

Prothoüs   A Greek leader in the Trojan War who came from the region of Mount Pelion,★ in Thessaly★ (Greece).

Pylos   See Nestor.

Pyrrha   "The Fiery One"; wife of Deucalion.★ After the Great Flood, she and Deucalion regenerated the human race by throwing stones over their shoulders: those thrown by Deucalion became men, those thrown by Pyrrha became women.

Pyrrhus   Son of Achilles★ and Deidamia (whom Achilles raped on the island of Scyros;)★ killer of Priam★ and symbol of Greek brutality during the destruction of Troy.★

Python   A snake which inhabited Mount Parnassus, in Greece, and which was killed by Phoebus★ (Apollo) before he set up his oracle at Delphi.

Rhesus   See Diomedes (1).

Rhipaean Mountains   A more or less mythical mountain range in central Europe beyond which the people especially loved by Phoebus,★ the Hyperboreans (those who live beyond Boreas,★ the north wind), supposedly lived in a kind of earthly paradise.

Rhoeteum   A headland jutting into the sea not far from Troy,★ and the town on that headland.

Rioni   The modern name of the river Phasis★ (in the USSR), on which Colchis,★ home of Medea,★ was situated.

Salamis   An island off the coast of Attica,★ in the Saronic Gulf.

Sarmatians   Nomadic Slavic people living in parts of what is now the western Soviet Union and part of Eastern Europe, between the Vistula and the Don; culturally related to the Scythians.★

Scarphe   A small town in central Greece.

Sciron's Rocks   Precipitous cliffs between Athens and Megara; named for the bandit Sciron, who kicked passers-by into the sea from them. Sciron was killed by Theseus.★

Scylla   A voracious female seamonster with many doglike heads who lay in wait for sailors. Her traditional site in the works of later Greek and Roman writers is off the Sicilian coast. See Pelorus.

Scyros   An island off the coast of Euboea (Greece), where Thetis★ hid Achilles★ from Greek recruiters who wanted him to fight at Troy.★ See Achilles.

Scythians   Nomadic people of eastern Europe and Asia whom the Romans knew mostly from contacts in the areas adjoining the Black Sea; rendered as "Cossacks" in the translation. See Sarmatians.

Seres   The Chinese.

Sidonian   (1) Of Sidon in Phoenicia (modern Lebanon), or of a city colonized by the Phoenicians, such as Carthage (in Tunis) or Thebes★ (in Greece). (2) Colored with the crimson murex dye for which the Phoenicians were famous.

Sigeum   A town near Rhoeteum★ and Troy,★ in Asia Minor (Turkey).

Sinis   A bandit who lived on the Isthmus of Corinth.★ He tied passing travelers between two bent pine trees, which he then released; when the trees sprang apart, the victim was torn in half. He was killed by Theseus.★

Sinon   A Greek spy who persuaded the Trojans to take the Wooden Horse into Troy.

Sirens   Mermaid-like singers whose beautiful voices lured sailors to destruction. Enchanted by the Sirens' song and eager to find its source, sailors were drawn off course to a shore where they crashed on treacherous rocks.

Sisyphus   Son of Aeolus★; king of Corinth★, famous for his ability to tell lies; condemned after death to roll a stone up a mountainside forever in retribution for his crimes.

Sol   The (god of the) Sun. See Phoebus.

Sparta   A city in the Peloponnesus.

Stymphalian birds   Mythical birds whose feathers were lethal shafts; killed by Hercules.★

Styx   (1) An allegedly poisonous river in the Peloponnesus. (2) The most famous of the rivers of the dead in Greco-Roman myth. An oath sworn by the Styx was binding even on the gods.

Suebians   A Germanic tribe living east of the Elbe and known for its practice of human sacrifice.

Sunion   A promontory on the coast of Attica.★ It was here, in some versions of the myth, that Aegeus★ kept watch for the return of his son Theseus★ from Crete and the Minotaur. When Aegeus saw the black sails of the returning ship (Theseus had forgotten to change them), he assumed his son was dead and threw himself into the sea, thereafter known as the Aegean. A famous temple of Neptune★ (Poseidon) was later built on the promontory.

Symplegades   Mythical rocks in the sea which stood apart and separate until a moving object tried to pass between them, at which time they clashed together. The *Argo*★ had to sail through them. After its safe passage, the rocks remained apart and never clashed together again.

Syrtes   Traditionally treacherous shallows off the coast of Tunis, in the Gulf of Sidra.

Taenarum   A cave in the southern Peloponnesus through which Hercules★ dragged Cerberus★ out of the underworld; one of the traditional entrances/exits of the underworld. See Avernus.

Talthybius   A Greek messenger. In the manuscripts he is the messenger only for the appearance of Achilles'★ ghost in *Trojan Women*, but it makes sense to give him the lines simply marked *nuntius*, "messenger," too.

Tanais   The Don River.

Tantalus   A king of Lydia (in Asia Minor [Turkey]); the son of Jupiter;★ a wealthy and criminal ruler who sacrificed and cooked his own son, Pelops,★ as a banquet for the gods. For his sins Tantalus was punished in one of two ways, according to various authors: (1) He was imprisoned in the underworld, where he was forced to stand in flowing water up to his neck, with grape clusters hanging above his head. Whenever he reached up to eat or down to drink, the grapes and the water receded beyond his reach. (2) He was left in constant fear of a stone poised over his head, forever about to fall. His daughter was Niobe.★

Tartarus   The deepest pit of the underworld, where the most terrible criminals are punished; it was guarded by the dog Cerberus.★

Taurus   A mountain range running inland from Lycia, in southwest Turkey. In Latin the name is suggestive of *taurus*, "bull," and the zodiacal sign Taurus.

Taygetus   A mountain range near Sparta.★

Telemachus   Son of Ulysses.★

Telephus   Son of Hercules★ and Auge, the daughter of a king of Arcadia★ (Greece); he eventually became king of Mysia,★ in Asia Minor (Turkey). His city was attacked by Achilles★ and the Greeks, who mistook it for Troy,★ and Telephus was wounded by Achilles. The only (and paradoxical) cure for the wound proved to be the rust from the spear that had wounded him. (Thus Pyrrhus★ can claim that Achilles' weapons cure as well as kill.)

Tempe   A valley in Thessaly★ (Greece).

Tenedos   An island off the coast of Troy,★ plundered by Achilles.★

Tethys   Wife of Oceanus;★ mother of Thetis,★ and thus grandmother of Achilles.★ If Ceres★ is a kind of Mother Earth, Tethys is a kind of Mother Ocean.

Teucer   Father of Dardanus★ and ultimate ancestor of the Trojan royal house.

Thebes   (1) A city of Boeotia (Greece), founded by a Phoenician explorer and exile, Cadmus; home of the prophet and Argonaut Mopsus.★ (2) A city in Asia Minor, home of Andromache.★

Thermodon   A river near the Black Sea, best known for its associations with the Amazons.★

Theseus   Son of Neptune★ or Aegeus;★ stepson of Medea;★ famous as a killer of monsters in and around Attica★ (see Marathon; Procrustes; Sciron's Rocks; Sinis). Later he went to Crete, where he killed the Minotaur. He left Crete with Ariadne,★ daughter of Minos,★ but abandoned her on the island of Naxos. On his return to Athens he neglected to change the black sails on his ship, and Aegeus,★ interpreting them as a sign of his son's death, committed suicide (see Sunion). Theseus fought and defeated the Amazons★ and married their queen, Antiope,★ by whom he had a son, Hippolytus.★ He later married Ariadne's sister, Phaedra.★ Theseus is often treated by ancient writers as a semihistorical figure (as in Plutarch's *Lives*, where, as founder of the Athenian state, he is paired with the legendary founder of Rome, Romulus).

Thessaly   A region of north-central Greece, in which Jason's★ hometown of Iolcos★ is situated. Thessaly is also famous as the home of Achilles,★ who was born and raised there by the centaur Chiron.★ It is no less famous for its horses (and centaurs), and for its magic and witches. For many Roman writers, Thessaly is also ominous as the site of the battle of Pharsalia (48 B.C.), where Julius Caesar defeated the republican armies under Pompey.★

Thetis   Mother of Achilles★ and wife of Peleus.★

Thrace   A mountainous and barbaric area in what is now the border regions of Greece, Bulgaria, and Turkey. Its northern boundary was the river Danube, and it was bisected by the river Haemus.★ In Seneca's day only the part south of the Haemus was, strictly speaking, Thrace. The northern area was the province of Moesia. Thrace was the home of Orpheus.★

Thria   A lowland community in western Attica,★ near Eleusis.★

Thule   Probably Iceland.

Thyestes   See Atreus.

Tigris   A river running through present-day Turkey and Iraq; for all practical purposes, the easternmost limit of Roman influence in Seneca's day.

Tiphys   The helmsman of the *Argo*.★

Titan   (1) Sol★ (the Sun). (2) One of a family of giants who ruled the earth until their defeat by Jupiter★ and the Olympians, who imprisoned them under Mount Aetna.★

Titaressos   A river in Thessaly★ (Greece) which flows into the river Peneus. Seneca seems to think it flows into the Aegean.

Tityos   A son of Earth who attempted to rape Leto, the mother of Phoebus★ (Apollo) and Diana.★ He was punished in the underworld by having his ever-regenerating liver eaten by two vultures.

Tonans   The Thunderer (Jupiter).★

Trachis   A town in central Greece under the control of Achilles'★ family.

Tricce   A town in Thessaly★ (Greece).

Triptolemus   A hero of Eleusis,★ linked with the cult of Ceres★ and Proserpina.★

Tritons   Minor (and musical) sea divinites.

Troezen   A town on the east coast of the Peloponnesus.

Troy   A city on the Hellespont, twice conquered by the Greeks: first under
Hercules,★ who was angered by the bad faith of its king, Laomedon,★ and then, in the next generation (when Laomedon's son
Priam★ was king), by Agamemnon★ and a coalition of Greek leaders. The conquest was precipitated by the abduction of the Greek
queen Helen,★ wife of Agamemnon's brother Menelaus,★ by
Paris,★ son of Priam. Roman writers felt a special sympathy for
the Trojans in their wars with the Greeks because of the tradition
that Troy's founders originally came from Italy and that the Romans
could trace their own ethnic origins to a refugee (Aeneas) who
escaped from the second and catastrophic defeat of Troy by the
Greeks (see Venus). It was rumored in the last half of the first
century B.C. that Rome's Caesars intended to transfer the capital
of the empire to a rebuilt Troy.

Tyndareus   King of Sparta;★ in some versions, father of Helen★ and her
sister Clytemnestra, and of Castor★ and Pollux.★ Helen is often
referred to as "daughter of Tyndareus."

Typhoeus   A monstrous, hundred-headed son of Earth who fought against
Jupiter★ for control of the heavens; defeated and buried under
Mount Aetna.★

Tyre   A city of Phoenicia (Lebanon), famous for its high living and its
crimson dyes. See Sidonian.

Ulysses   Son of Laertes;★ the Roman Odysseus, generally treated unfavor-
ably in Latin poetry because of his treacherous behavior, but presented as an exemplar of the suffering hero, worthy of comparison
with Cato and Socrates, in Roman prose. The contrast is particularly
sharp in Seneca: the Ulysses of *Trojan Women* is one of ancient
tragedy's most villainous characters, but the Ulysses of Seneca's
prose works is the embodiment of Stoic virtue.

Venus   Beautiful but faithless goddess of love; wife of Vulcan★ and lover
of Mars;★ mother of Amor★ (Cupid)★ and, in Roman tradition,
divine forebear of the Caesars because of their mythical descent
from Aeneas, Venus' son by Anchises, a Trojan prince. In Latin
the word *venus* often means essentially sexuality, even the sexual
act.

Vulcan   The smelter of metals (Mulciber, in Latin); god of metalworking
and fire, associated with volcanoes, especially Mount Aetna;★ husband of Venus.★

Xanthus   The main river in the vicinity of Troy.★

Zacynthos   An Ionian★ island near Cephallenia★ and Ithaca.★

Zephyr   The west wind; wind of springtime.

Zetes   See Boreas; Calais.

Library of Congress Cataloging-in-Publication Data

Seneca, Lucius Annaeus, ca. 4 B.C.–65 A.D.
  Medea.

  (Masters of Latin literature)
    1. Medea (Greek mythology)—Drama.   I.   Ahl, Frederick
M.   II. Title.   III. Series.
PA6666.M4A45   1986   872'.01   86-47635
ISBN 0-8014-9432-X (alk. paper)